PERMISSIVE RESIDENTS

WEST PAPUAN REFUGEES LIVING IN
PAPUA NEW GUINEA

PERMISSIVE RESIDENTS

WEST PAPUAN REFUGEES LIVING IN PAPUA NEW GUINEA

DIANA GLAZEBROOK

MONOGRAPHS IN
ANTHROPOLOGY SERIES

ANU
THE AUSTRALIAN NATIONAL UNIVERSITY

E PRESS

ANU

E PRESS

Published by ANU E Press
The Australian National University
Canberra ACT 0200, Australia
Email: anuepress@anu.edu.au
This title is also available online at: http://epress.anu.edu.au/permissive_citation.html

National Library of Australia
Cataloguing-in-Publication entry

Author:	Glazebrook, Diana.
Title:	Permissive residents : West Papuan refugees living in Papua New Guinea / Diana Glazebrook.
ISBN:	9781921536229 (pbk.) 9781921536236 (online)
Subjects:	Ethnology--Papua New Guinea--East Awin. Refugees--Papua New Guinea--East Awin. Refugees--Papua (Indonesia)
Dewey Number:	305.8009953

Cover design by ANU E Press.

Dedicated to the memory of
Arnold Ap (1 July 1945 – 26 April 1984) and
Marthen Rumabar (d. 2006).

Table of Contents

List of Illustrations

Photos:

Photo 1. Yospan dancing accompanied by Mambesak musicians in front of the Governor's Office, Jayapura (Kapissa is the spectacled dancer facing the photographer, and Ap is second guitarist from right), c.1981. (Chapter 2)

Photo 2. Arnold Ap (seated fourth from the right) and fellow Mambesak musicians, c. 1981. (Chapter 2)

Photo 3. Grating cassava to become like sago. (Chapter 7)

Photo 4. 'Who's [sic] put the border mark!' Oil painting by Herry Offide, 1999. (Chapter 9)

Photo 5. Decorated wall, entry area of house at Waraston camp, East Awin. (Chapter 10)

Maps:

Map 1. Location of East Awin. (Prologue)

Map 2. Irian Jaya and the border region of Papua New Guinea showing the location of Cenderawasih University (UNCEN), Jayapura, East Awin, and regions from where Ap recorded performance material. (Chapter 2)

Acknowledgements

The manuscript for this book was written during a post-doctoral research fellowship awarded by the Centre for Cross-Cultural Research at The Australian National University 2003–04. It evolved out of a PhD dissertation written in the Department of Anthropology, Research School of Pacific and Asian Studies, ANU, during the period 1996-2001. The original dissertation was guided by the insights and analyses of a panel of three advisors, Kathryn Robinson, Sjoerd Jaarsma and Chris Ballard. Others who read single chapters carefully and offered important comments include George Aditjondro, Michael Cookson, Stuart Kirsch, and JW Schoorl. George Aditjondro provided access to many unpublished resources that were critical to the chapter on Arnold Ap. I was also privileged to have Pim Schoorl map watersheds in the Muyu region. Justine FitzGerald read the whole dissertation, generously correcting my translations from Indonesian into English. Father Jacques Gros, who lives and works among Muyu in the border camps of PNG, read the dissertation and this book, and contributed valuable ethnographic comments.

Glossary

ABRI	Indonesian Armed Forces
bilum	string bag
dusun	*dusun* is an Indonesian term used by West Papuans to mention a bounded area of land that has been passed down from fathers to sons for many generations, containing cultivated areas such as rubber, coconut and rambutan plantings, naturally occurring and planted sago gardens, forested areas for hunting, as well as rivers and rockpools. Ancestors are buried in their dusun, and the spirits of some continue to occupy it. A person's history and that of their lineage is inscribed in the features of their *dusun*.
merdeka	political independence, can also mean freedom and liberation
OPM	Free Papua Movement
PEPERA	PEPERA is the abbreviation of *Penentuan Pendapat Rakyat* referred to popularly as the Act of Free Choice. Between 14 July and 2 August 1969, 1022 West Papuan delegates appointed by the Indonesian administration voted in a series of regional consultations on Irian Jaya's political integration into Indonesia.
translokal	From 1976, where disputes occurred over land rights caused by transmigration, local peoples were to be compensated for the appropriation of their land by being incorporated into the transmigration program as local transmigrants known as *translokal*.
Transmigration	A central government project to relocate landless and underemployed families from densely populated areas like Java and Madura to areas considered underpopulated such as Kalimantan and the Indonesian Province of Papua.
UNCEN	Cenderawasih University, Jayapura
UNHCR	United Nations High Commission for Refugees
WPIA	West Papuan Indigenous People's Association

A note on transcription and terms

'Northerner' is a term that I have borrowed from the refugee expression *orang utara* referring to people from the northern region, including those from the north-west coast (Sorong, Manokwari) and the islands (Biak-Numfoor, Serui), as well as those people living inland of Jayapura at Genyem and other places. The term northerner stands in contrast to 'southerner' (*orang selatan*), referring broadly to Muyu, Mandobo and Kanum peoples at Iowara. Usually, highlanders from the Jayawijaya mountain range were identified as 'Dani people' (*orang Dani*) or 'mountain people' (*orang gunung*). People at Iowara who came from the Oksibil region near the Star Mountains were also called *orang gunung*.

Several terms appeared frequently in conversation in the field, and throughout the book. I have translated *perjuangan* as 'the struggle', meaning the political struggle for nationhood. *Pembebasan* is translated as 'liberation' or 'freedom' although it was occasionally used by narrators to represent a state of political independence. *Asli* is translated as 'indigenous' or 'original'. *Asing* is translated as 'foreign', and *pendatang* as 'newcomer'. *Tabah* (or *pertabahan*) is translated as 'endure' or 'holding out', for example in the context of holding out in exile.

Prologue

Intoxicating flag

Since 1961, West Papuan people in the 'Indonesian Province' of Papua raising the Morning Star flag in public have been shot by Indonesian soldiers.[1] Public declarations of allegiance to West Papuan nationhood broadcast beneath the flag have provoked violent retaliation. Raising the flag in public recalls the nascent state. It acts to constitute a West Papuan people and place, momentarily establishing the legitimacy of an alternative regime outside of the Indonesian state.[2] While West Papuan people at the East Awin refugee settlement in Papua New Guinea (PNG) no longer fear being shot down for raising the flag, the affect is not dissimilar. Raising the West Papuan flag is intoxicating. In the moments between the flag's ascension from the bottom of the pole to the top, the air can be cut with a knife. Acts of flag raising have constituted 'signal events' in the history of West Papua since 1961.

At East Awin, flag-raising ceremonies are held annually to commemorate several events: the inaugural raising of the Morning Star as a national flag by the West New Guinea Council (1 December 1961); the first physical battle between the OPM or Free Papua Movement and the Indonesian military at Arfai (28 July 1965); Seth Rumkorem's Declaration of Independence (1 July 1971); and the failed uprising in Jayapura (11 February 1984). In the second month of my dissertation fieldwork at the former United Nations Commissioner for Refugees (UNHCR) refugee settlement in East Awin in 1998, I received a hand-written invitation to attend the flag-raising ceremony on 1 July. The ceremony took place at Waraston, East Awin, a camp comprised of people from the north coast and adjacent islands. A ceremonial ground was freshly scythed for the occasion, a flagpole erected, and a stage covered in tarpaulin. The ceremonial ground formed part of a narrow swathe cut through the surrounding jungle. To the south it bordered a clay track that wound its way past Waraston, and continued for 10 kilometres in both directions past 17 other small camps. On the northern side of the ceremonial field were the houses of Waraston. These 20 houses were perched on 2-metre poles, and constructed from milled and hand-adzed timber. Roofs were a bricolage of weathered plastic sheeting, and odd bits of bark, tin and sago thatch.

I was invited with several other people to sit in the makeshift stage lined with blue tarpaulin. Other guests shifted in their seats alongside me, fanned themselves and picked the biting insects off their legs. Next to me sat Lucia, a dignified widow whose husband had been shot by Indonesian soldiers in the forest on the border, and then burned alive in the house into which he had crawled. (Note:

all names of West Papuans in this book, except those of songwriters, are pseudonyms.) Yohanes sat with his back to Lucia and me. A feisty war veteran who had fought the first West Papuan battle against the Indonesians at Arfai in 1965, he had sustained injuries to his spine after being captured and beaten with a plank. His tensed back reminded me of the embodied character of the struggle. Seated behind three low tables at the front of the stage were several lay preachers and teachers.

One side of the ceremonial field was lined with women holding babies folded into fabric slings. They used umbrellas to shade themselves against the fierce morning sun. Young girls stood near their mothers, minding infant siblings whose faces had been dusted with talcum powder. Men stood at attention some distance from the women and girls, following a military drill directed from the podium. Three young men designated as flag-bearers delicately performed the ritual of unfolding and raising the flag with white-gloved hands. The speakers wore camouflage garb, the uniform of their jungle-based resistance. Impassioned speeches were read about Dutch preparation of the West Papuan nation-state, annexation by Indonesia, and the struggle since 1962 to restore nationhood. With voices resonant with emotion, men and women and children sang the seven-verse song Hai Tanahku Papua (O, My Land Papua). Adopted as the national anthem on 1 December 1961, following a vote by the West New Guinea Council, the sensuous lyrics invoke the West Papuan nation's homeland imagined as a geographic and territorial entity, of coastal, lowland and highland settings:

> O, My Land Papua
> My land of birth
> Thou should I love 'til my dying day

> I love the white beaches
> That colour thy coasts
> Where the blue waters
> Glisten in the sun

> I love the sounds of the waves
> The breaks on thy beaches
> The songs that always
> Gladden my heart

> I love thy mountains
> Lofty and great
> And the clouds that drift
> Around thy tops

I love thee thy forests
That cover the land
And I love to roam
Under the shady green

I love thee thy land
With thy resources
To pay for my cleverness
And for my work

Thank thee O, Lord
For the Land of thy gift
Make me also diligent
To convey thy aims

(Translated by Tom Ireeuw at Blackwara camp, Vanimo in 1984.)

After the ceremony I joined a line of people that crossed the main jungle track to a small cemetery at the side of the Providence Lutheran church. Here we scattered yellow petals over the grave of a young architect from Biak, who had been knifed in the marketplace at East Awin by another West Papuan refugee who was said to have lost his mind.

At dusk, people reassembled to witness the ceremonial lowering and folding of the flag, and its solemn presentation to the master of ceremonies. Afterwards the line of onlookers dissolved, and drifted towards an old schoolhouse where women served sweet black tea with steamed buns called *bapauw*, and rainbow cake. Later, men played cards on the low tables on the stage lit by kerosene pressure lanterns. Young people danced Yospan to music cassettes sent by relatives from Jayapura. (Yospan was chosen as Irian Jaya's official provincial dance at a seminar convened by the regional government in the 1980s.) Leaning against the schoolhouse wall admiring the dancers, I struck up a conversation with the woman standing next to me. She proceeded to reveal the biographical details of several women who were dancing or watching the dance. One woman's father was serving life imprisonment in Kalisosok prison, Java. A woman nursing her baby was the daughter-in-law of the freedom movement leader who made the independence declaration in 1971. The dance was accompanied by *misteri hidup* or the mystery of life, a song composed in prison by musician Arnold Ap in the days before his execution. The woman told me that the movements of this dance mimicked the paddling of a canoe, but young people at East Awin had never seen a sea canoe. Nor had they seen the ocean. She told me that northerners perceived the East Awin settlement as a sort of living hell: an inland lowland swamp distant from the sweeping white beaches pounded by waves and fringed by palms. Their previous coastal diet of bountiful seafood, coconut, sago and

3

garden produce had been replaced by the cassava plant at East Awin. They processed its flesh to resemble sago and boiled its leaves to eat as greens.

Although hand-written invitations to commemorative ceremonies were issued to each camp at East Awin, the audience was usually comprised of northerners from Waraston camp only. A Waraston woman explained to me:

> We share this matter of the struggle so people should participate—it is not just [for] us from Waraston. Yet they don't know the design of the flag or the lyrics of the anthem. In the past they have joined in, but not any more. A kind of despair, they say there is no result. They laugh at us.

At Waraston, the flagpole, stage and audience faced the road, the main thoroughfare at East Awin. During the flag-raising ceremony that day, and on subsequent occasions, I observed people from neighbouring camps returning from the market along this road. They halted, and waited without lowering their laden billum until a group had collected, then walked slowly past in single file—without so much as turning their faces towards the ceremony. According to the organisers, other people at East Awin considered flag-raising commemorative ceremonies to be a political activity that contested the conditions of their refugee and 'permissive residency' status, risking their deportation.

In the performance of national rituals containing flag raising, anthem singing and historical speeches, these refugees constitute their identity as West Papuans. At East Awin, even mentioning the Morning Star flag elicits historical monologues about West Papuan experiences of the atrocities of Indonesian colonisation. It is not just the flag and anthem that bring out narratives about Indonesian colonisation though. In this book I examine other events, campaigns and policies that invoke a similar reaction, for example, transmigration, the 1969 Penentuan Pendapat Rakyat (PEPERA) or Act of Free Choice, the *koteka* campaign and Arnold Ap. Individually, and sometimes in confluence, these events, campaigns and policies caused some West Papuans to seek political asylum across the border in PNG.

The performance of national rituals at East Awin needs foregrounding in a brief chronology of events in the Indonesian province of Papua since 1961. These events provide a backdrop to the cross-border movement of West Papuans into PNG. Each event led to government and military policies deemed oppressive, provoking resistance referred to as the struggle to attain *merdeka* or West Papuan independence.[3] On 1 December 1961, the Dutch administration of Netherlands New Guinea oversaw the election of a New Guinea Council, and installation of the ordinances of nation-statehood like a territorial flag and national anthem. On 19 December, Indonesian President Sukarno declared a campaign of total mobilisation to wrest Netherlands New Guinea from the Dutch. Dutch control of Netherlands New Guinea was subsequently ceded to Indonesia through the New York Agreement on 15 August 1962, which provided for a United Nations (UN) transitional authority present until 1 May 1963. Between 14 July and 2 August 1969, West Papuans voted in eight assemblies (1022 delegates appointed by the Indonesian administration) in the Act of Free Choice, and West Irian was declared Indonesia's seventeenth province.[4] The Indonesian government's military actions and policies, implemented since 1962 to secure West Papua as part of the republic, have led to land annexation, internal displacement, deaths in custody and the killing of unarmed villagers and independence supporters.

It was a chance reading of these events, as chronicled by George Monbiot in his travelogue *Poisoned arrows,* that first aroused my interest in West Papua as a possible dissertation subject in 1995. Further reading on the demise of Arnold Ap, variously described as an anthropologist, museum curator, musician and composer, increased my resolve. In 1996, getting permission from the government of Indonesia to do anthropological fieldwork in West Papua could mean years of waiting without a positive result. In mid-1997, while studying Indonesian in Jogjakarta, Java, I visited the families of fellow West Papuan students at Gajah Mada University. I lived in neighbourhoods in Jayapura, Biak and Wamena; sites where some of the 'signal events' in the history of West Papua had occurred. With only a slim possibility of getting permission to do fieldwork in West Papua, I decided to apply for a research visa from the government of PNG to do twelve months' fieldwork at East Awin, a former UNHCR refugee settlement for West Papuans that had been established in 1989.

Between 1984–86, as many as 11,000 West Papuans crossed into PNG seeking asylum (between 1962 and 1969, the Australian Administration of PNG recorded around 4,000 crossings by West Papuans).[5] Pushed by particular forces in their local area—often battles between Indonesian soldiers and West Papuan freedom fighters—they crossed at different times, as individuals and in groups, in a multitude of places along the international border. Movement can be broadly categorised on the basis of shared place of origin and crossing point, in terms of four relatively discreet phases. I refer to the people who crossed the border to seek asylum during the period 1984–86 in terms of four groups: 'northerners', Dani, Muyu and Sota peoples.

The first major movement comprised about 1000 northerners who crossed the border near Vanimo between February and June 1984. This northerner group included formally educated and politically active people from north-coast towns (Jayapura, Sorong and Manokwari) and islands (Biak-Numfoor and Serui), as well as villagers from the northern border region. At Vanimo these northerners were housed in a resettlement camp called Blackwater. A second movement occurred in 1985 when about 350 Dani from the Baliem Valley crossed near Bewani, south of Vanimo. This group was also relocated to Blackwater. Both of these movements occurred in PNG's northern Sandaun Province. A third movement occurred during an 18-month period between April 1984 and September 1985 when 9500 Muyu crossed the border into Western Province at numerous crossing points. A fourth movement took place in 1992 when about 100 families from the border town of Sota sought refuge across the border in the Morehead District, PNG. (In December 2000, after the period of fieldwork, a fifth major movement occurred when about 400 people from the Baliem Valley, who were living in and around the capital Jayapura, crossed the border near Vanimo and sought asylum.)

After the government of PNG acceded to the UN Convention and Protocol Relating to the Status of Refugees in 1986, it determined that West Papuans would be relocated from 17 informal camps on the international border to a single inland location as recommended by UNHCR.[6] The government identified a 6000-hectare site at East Awin, a division of the Kiunga District in Western Province, approximately 120 kilometres east of the Indonesian–PNG border. At the time of research for this book in 1998–89, East Awin settlement consisted of 17 'camps' stretched along the Kiunga–Nomad road between 40 to 70 kilometres. The population was approximately 3500 or 20 people per square kilometre, compared to less than 10 people per square kilometre in neighbouring areas.[7]

During the period of fieldwork at East Awin (March to September 1998 and February to September 1999), most West Papuan refugees were either applying for permissive residency in PNG, or planning to repatriate to West Papua. The offer and processing of permissive residency permits, and preparation for repatriation by a large faction at East Awin, occurred somewhat fortuituously during the period of my fieldwork. Activities associated with permissive residency and repatriation allowed me to hone my understanding of refugee-ness; specifically, what it meant to be a West Papuan refugee in relation to being a repatriate, or permissive resident. As this book elaborates, remaining a refugee or becoming a repatriate or permissive resident was determined in part by people's subjective engagement with 'national' history, and their pragmatism at a household and/or village level.

Map 1. Location of East Awin

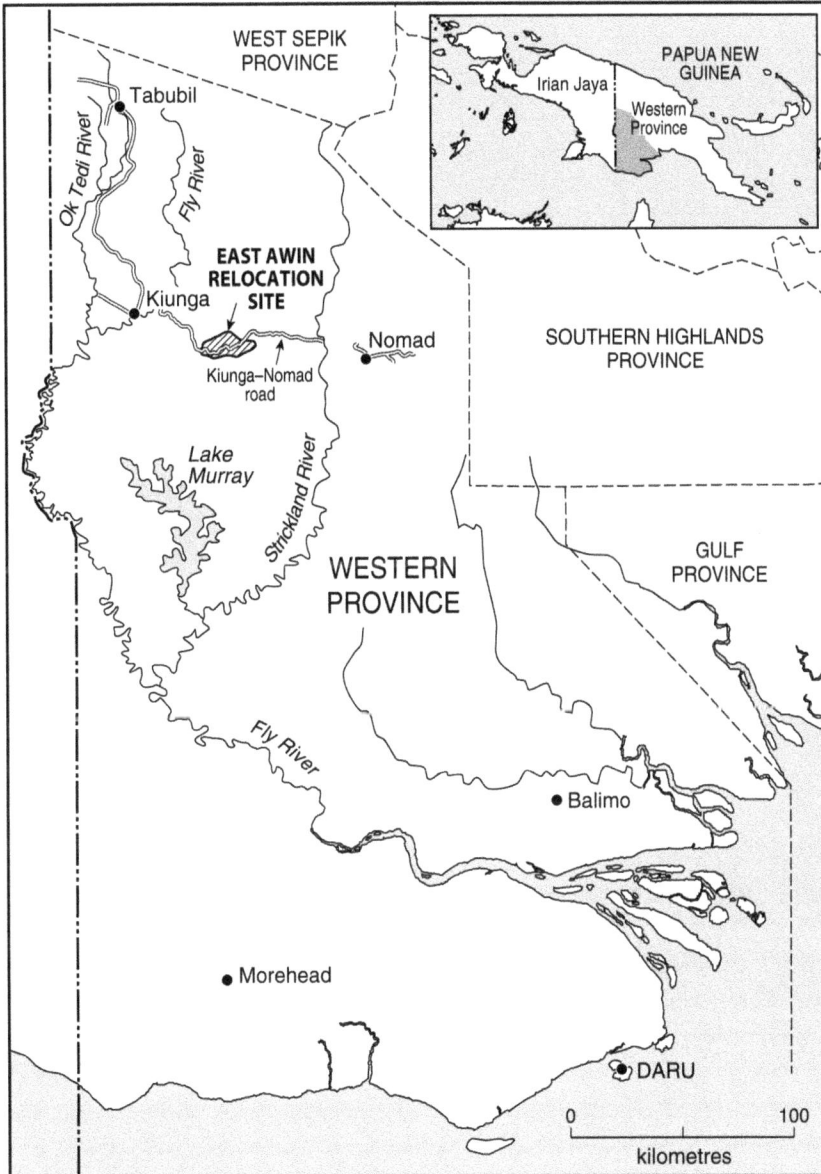

Map: Cartographic Services, Research School of Pacific and Asian Studies, College of Asia and the Pacific, The Australian National University.

This book begins by unpacking the narratives of colonisation told by West Papuans at Awin which provide an historical and political backdrop to resistance, and to their own cross-border flight and subsequent claims for asylum. In the narratives of colonisation contained in the first chapter, the 'canonisation' of 'Indonesians' is discernible.[8] By canonisation, I borrow from Malkki to refer to the way that atrocity against a category can lead to the creation of boundaries and classification of the agents or perpetrators as essentially inhuman.[9] The agents of civilian policies and military campaigns mentioned above were soldiers and civil servants—Indonesian citizens. Spontaneous migrants and government-assisted transmigrants total almost 50 per cent of the Irian Jaya population. Theological scholars propose that atrocities against West Papuans as a category have generated collective 'memories of suffering' or *memoria passionis*.[10] These collective memories effect antagonistic opposition, but their latent energy can potentially 'turn the existing status quo upside down.'[11] Malkki and Anderson call this 'inversion', and suggest that canonising behaviour risks the inversion of primordial nationalism.[12] Hypothetically, in an independent state of West Papua, Indonesians could experience surveillance, control and possibly even expulsion. But it is not inevitable that ethnic conflict will be generated by primordial sentiment, and researchers have shown ethnic violence to be generated by the state to appear like primordialism, and to be linked to developments in provincial and national politics.[13]

State atrocity against a category of people can lead to the creation of boundaries. In the context of West Papua, cultural performance as a boundary-making activity is most explicit in the work of museum curator and musician Arnold Ap, and the subject of the second chapter. During the 1969 Act of Free Choice voting period, Ap led a demonstration of fellow Cenderawasih University students and was imprisoned at the Gunung Ifar prison near Jayapura. Following his release, it is said that Ap made a conscious decision to mobilise West Papuan people in the preservation of their cultural identity through performance. Taking cultural difference as his 'conscious object',[14] Ap's work was directed towards cultural salvage, regeneration, and expression, rather than a racist project to dominate or eliminate non-Papuan groups. That is not to say that Ap's work did not 'musically feed the imagination'[15] of West Papuan nationhood. In his work as curator, composer and musician, Ap used performance to articulate cultural difference towards a contrastive or 'alternative identity'.[16] Memory of the suffering of Arnold Ap—who died at the hands of Indonesian soldiers—remains central to a *memoria passionis* of West Papuans, outside and inside the homeland. Ap's work has particular resonance at East Awin, where some of his fellow musicians and peers lived after crossing the border into PNG in 1984.

Paths of flight by West Papuans crossed various boundaries, and illuminate different experiences of displacement. Some such paths are elaborated in chapter three. The journey for northerners and Muyu people was shorter than for Dani highlanders. Dani people fled the Baliem Valley to seek refuge over the mountains to the north, in the lowland swamps of the Mamberamo basin. Although they were only 'internally displaced' among Mamberamo, their sense of displacement is signified by a landscape that is grotesque in its foreignness. It is terrifying, and produces famine for them. Lack of cultural knowledge means they cannot process foods like sago and coconut, and do not recognise forest food. In contrast, for Muyu people whose land lies contiguous to the international border, the familiarity of the landscape at East Awin, proximate to their own region and ancestral land known as *dusun*, amplifies their experience of displacement. For coastal and island northerners, it is the inland location of East Awin that is profoundly disorienting and unsettling. Deprivations experienced during the intense drought and bushfires in 1997 consolidated refugee perception and experience of East Awin as a dystopian place.

The movement of West Papuan people across the border into PNG, onto the other half of the island, affects a geographical and cultural space that appears small. The displacement of Muyu from their own land, occurring in the smallest of geographic and cultural spaces, is the subject of chapter four. By capturing the texture of Muyu displacement, I join other refugee researchers in challenging the assumption that movement inside a region requires less cultural adjustment because refugees are living with their own people or neighbours, in the same ecological landscape, on the other side of a colonial-imposed boundary.[17] Arjun Appadurai's concept of 'locality' as the production of new social spaces that generate other social spaces provides a useful framework to consider a process of social formation at East Awin, both in individual camps and across the settlement as a whole.[18] Chapter five examines social formation through various practices including fictive kinship, death and burial of close relatives and friends, and evolution of camps as bases of alliance.

Chapter six demonstrates the way that over time, the 'empty rainforest' at East Awin has become 'inscribed'[19] with refugees' own histories through such house- and garden-making activities as clearing, planting, harvesting, building and renovating. Casey's theorising of 'dwelling' as a conscious activity that can affect familiarity, and his notion of 'inhabiting' a space through certain body habits, offer insights into a process of resettlement.[20] Even at East Awin where people did not want to imagine settling in the medium term, many people prepared their environment to mitigate against feeling unsettled. Chapter seven describes how, among Muyu, sago consumption was the most concrete marker of their displacement at East Awin. They resisted becoming settled in the long term by refusing to plant sago. Yet they also tried to simulate sago flour by processing cassava, and tried to replicate sago thatch by curing (smoking) other thatch materials. Using Baudrillard's notion of simulation and 'dissimulation',[21] I explore the Muyu judgement that a sago appetite cannot be sated by cassava.

In spite of the dwelling, inhabiting and simulating activities of refugees at East Awin, the memory of their geographical place of origin, which is the place of their extended family and birthplace, is maintained intact as the real homeland. Return to the homeland is conceived in terms of a 'teleology of return'[22] —as something destined. Yet repatriation to the homeland may carry more risks than remaining in a dystopic place of resettlement. The first event of major repatriation occurred in 1993 when 94 families returned to Irian Jaya. Conrad's account of this repatriation event in chapter eight stands as a cautionary tale to prospective repatriates: repatriation risks becoming *translokal*. Conrad reveals how people's *dusun* was transformed into a transmigration settlement in their absence: partitioned rice paddies populated by Javanese farmers and retired military personnel. Repatriates were then integrated into this transmigration settlement as local transmigrants known as *translokal*. Becoming *translokal* in the event of repatriation realises West Papuan refugees' worst fear: that their ancestral land will be appropriated and they will become objects of the state. I consider the policy of *translokal* as a tactic of the state by drawing on Appadurai's exploration of neighbourhoods as subversive formations.[23]

Most West Papuans at East Awin chose not to repatriate, and applied for 'permissive residency'. Chapters nine and ten explain how this residency status removes their classification as refugees and, significantly, allows relocation elsewhere in PNG, and visiting rights to the homeland. In theory, at least, permissive residents have the opportunity to select a viable location of resettlement in PNG. They can relocate themselves to a place that is familiar both culturally and ecologically, and 'connected' to the geographic region of origin by telephone and/or transport. Relocation to a viable place that allows connection with kin and neighbours in the village or town of origin may radically affect people's experience of living outside the homeland.

Among West Papuan refugees at East Awin, a vision of teleological return to the geographical homeland continued at least until the end of my fieldwork research in 1999—which coincided with a short-lived period of political reformation across Indonesia. The largest repatriation event took place in 2000, involving 632 refugees, including 86 Dani. All repatriates were members of the West Papuan Indigenous People's Association. Chapter eleven explores the evolution of a discourse of indigeneity among these refugees, and tracks the fateful event of the return of the Dani group to the Baliem homeland. Then I shift from return to arrival, specifically, the arrival of 400 West Papuan asylum seekers at Vanimo in 2000. The relocation of this group from Vanimo to East Awin in October 2004 will augur a new era. The arrival of new refugees in the wake of others' departure, and their occupation of the vacant camp of repatriates, may cause those West Papuan refugees at East Awin who imagined their return to the geographical homeland to be imminent, to confront a different future.

ENDNOTES

[1] The island of New Guinea is shared by the country of Papua New Guinea (PNG) to the east, and to the west the 'Indonesian Province' of Papua, previously known as Netherlands New Guinea (to 1962), West Irian (1962–73), and Irian Jaya (1973–2001). In 2001, the name Irian Jaya was changed to Papua and ratified through the Special Autonomy Bill for Papua (Basic Law number 21 of 2001) by the Indonesian Parliament in Jakarta. In this book, people from the Indonesian Province of Papua living in PNG who have been categorised as refugees are referred to as 'West Papuan' as this is their preferred term, and one that distinguishes them as a nation rather than a provincial Indonesian ethnicity. When referring to territory, I use 'Indonesian Province' of Papua and 'Irian Jaya' depending on the period of reference. Both recognise the region's administration as a province of the Indonesian Republic since 1969. Where West Papuans refer to their homeland, I follow their own use of 'West Papua'.

[2] Danilyn Rutherford, 'Waiting for the end in Biak: violence, order and a flag raising', *Indonesia*, 67, 1999, p. 44.

[3] John Ondawame, ''One people one soul': West Papuan nationalism Organisasi Papua Merdeka (OPM)/Free Papua Movement', PhD thesis, The Australian National University, 2000.

[4] John Saltford, 'United Nations involvement with the act of self determination in West Irian (Indonesian West New Guinea) 1968 to 1969', *Indonesia*, 69, 2000.

[5] Alan Smith, 'Crossing the border: West Papuan refugees and self-determination of peoples', PhD thesis, Monash University, 1990; Rosemary Preston, 'Refugees in Papua New Guinea: government responses and assistance, 1984–1988', *International Migration Review*, 29, 3 (99), 1992, pp. 843–76.

[6] Rosemary Preston.

[7] B. J. Allen, et al. *Agricultural systems of Papua New Guinea Western Province: text summaries, maps, code lists and village identification*, Department of Human Geography, Research School of Pacific Studies, The Australian National University, Canberra, 1993.

[8] Theo P. A. Van den Brock and J. Budi Hernawan, *Memoria passionis di Papua: kondisi sosial-politik dan hak asasi manusia*, LSPP, Jakarta, 2001.

[9] Liisa Malkki, *Purity and exile: violence, memory and national cosmology among Hutu refugees in Tanzania*, University of Chicago Press, Chicago, 1995, p. 244.

[10] Van den Broek and Hernawan; Benny Giay, *Menuju Papua Baru: Beberapa pokok pikiran sekitar Emansipasi Orang Papua*. Seri Deiyai II. Deiyai/Els-ham Papua, Jayapura, 2000.

[11] Van den Broek and Hernawan.

[12] Malkki, p. 257; Benedict Anderson, *Imagined communities: reflections on the origins and spread of nationalism*, Verso, London, 1983, p. 136.

[13] For example, Octovianus Mote and Danilyn Rutherford, 'From Irian Jaya to Papua: the limits of primordialism in Indonesia's troubled east', *Indonesia*, 72, 2001.

[14] Arjun Appadurai, *Modernity at large: cultural dimensions of globalisation*, University of Minnesota Press, Minneapolis, 1996, p. 147.

[15] Greg Gow, *The Oromo in exile: from the horn of Africa to the suburbs of Australia*, Melbourne University Press, Melbourne, 2002, p. 56.

[16] Danilyn Rutherford, 'Remembering Sam Kapissa', *Inside Indonesia*, 67, 2001, pp. 16–17.

[17] B. E. Harrell-Bond and E. Voutira, 'Anthropology and the study of refugees', *Anthropology Today*, 8, 4, 1992, p. 7.

[18] Appadurai.

[19] Stuart Kirsch, 'The Yonggom of New Guinea: an ethnography of sorcery, ritual and magic', PhD thesis, University of Pennsylvania, 1991; Stuart Kirsch, 'Changing views of place and time along the Ok Tedi', in J. Weiner and A. Rumsey (eds), *Mining and indigenous lifeworlds in Australia and Papua New Guinea*, Sean Kingston Publisher, Oxon, 2004.

[20] E. S. Casey, *Getting back into place, toward a renewed understanding of the place world*, Indiana University Press, Bloomington, 1992, pp. 114–15, 117.

[21] Jean Baudrillard, *Simulacra and simulation*, translated by S. F. Glaser, University of Michigan Press, Ann Arbor, 1994, p. 3.

[22] James Clifford, *Routes: travel and translation in the late twentieth century*, Harvard University Press, Cambridge MA, 1997, p. 249.

[23] Appadurai, pp. 182–8.

Chapter 1

Speaking historically about West Papua

Indonesian administration of Irian Jaya was overseen by President Suharto from 1967 until his forced resignation on 21 May 1998. Under the leadership of then President Sukarno, it was Suharto who led the military campaign that 'liberated' Netherlands New Guinea from the Dutch (1961–66). Suharto's resignation resonated among West Papuans at East Awin. People were not jubilant, but the spirit or elan of the settlement lifted subtly. Not long after hearing the news of his downfall on my shortwave radio, I was visiting the house of Mientje, a middle-aged woman who worked as a nurse at the East Awin settlement hospital. Her neat house boasted shuttered windows and embroidered curtains, and a slat floor laid with dyed papyrus mats. A calendar hung from a roofing nail embedded in the wall. It was hand-drawn and consisted of a simple grid. Set at the month of May, the date 21 had been circled, and annotated 'Suharto *turun*'. Translating most simply as 'Suharto down', the note referred to Suharto's forced resignation. Mientje's austere reference undoubtedly concealed her elation.

The Indonesian military raid that had forced Mientje and her husband's flight from Irian Jaya had been violently sudden, forcing them to leave behind three children who were attending school in a nearby provincial town. Mientje recounted to me exactly how she had left her kitchen before fleeing: unwashed dishes in the kitchen sink, dinner plates on the table and her infant's blanket draped over the back of a kitchen chair. For Mientje, Suharto's resignation was nationally cathartic and affected her family's chance of return and reunion. The mobilisation of ordinary people across Indonesia in their demand for revolution in the months preceding Suharto's demise, together with a post-Suharto discourse of *reformasi* and *demokrasi*, was perceived by West Papuans at East Awin as auguring a new era of political change.

In the period following Suharto's demise, West Papuans at East Awin listened avidly to others speaking about the news. Only a handful of people in each camp owned a radio, and fewer still could afford batteries. People experimented with various techniques to prolong battery power: boiling them in water, burying them in plastic in warm soil, standing them upright in the sun, and even heating them in a frypan. In the East Awin High School where I taught conversational English to Grade 9 each morning, the off-duty teachers huddled around a radio in the staffroom, an iron-roofed, windowless shed with a packed clay floor. Tuned alternately to shortwave news from Jakarta, Melbourne and the Netherlands, the teachers updated each other and their neighbours about events occurring across the archipelago, and particularly in Irian Jaya. While elsewhere in Indonesia people protested in the streets about *krismon* or monetary crisis, in Irian Jaya the focus of protest was not *krismon* but experiences of colonisation.[1]

Villagers spoke about how their relatives had been killed by the Indonesian military, and their land had been appropriated by the state without compensation. Urban dwellers told of the way that migrants and transmigrants dominated the public and private sectors, and even the informal economy. The discourse of *demokrasi* in Irian Jaya was more than the freedom to articulate local testimony, it was also the opportunity for unprecedented political collectivity, activity and audience. A 'Team of One Hundred' West Papuan leaders met with President Habibie in 1999, and in the next year a Papua Presidium Council was elected, following a National Papuan Congress attended by 501 West Papuan delegates.

After Suharto's resignation, the candidacy of Sukarno's daughter Megawati Sukarnoputri for the Indonesian presidency became the subject of great speculation among West Papuans at East Awin. Some were entirely sceptical about her position in relation to Irian Jaya and viewed her as an expedient politician, like her father. Several older people read Megawati Sukarnoputri's candidacy in a period of *reformasi* in light of her father's annexation, which they believed to be a temporary custodianship. But perhaps these people had in mind Vice President Mohammad Hatta who, unlike Sukarno, had not fought for the inclusion of Netherlands New Guinea in the Declaration of Independence from the Dutch. As leader of the Indonesian Democratic Party of Struggle, Sukarnoputri became vice president under Abdurrahman Wahid in 1999, and was elevated to presidency from July 2001 until September 2004. Sukarnoputri's militaristic approach to Irian Jaya has been analysed as antithetical to Wahid's reformist one, and influenced by the Indonesian Armed Forces members of her party and cabinet, and her family's honour.[2] Sukarnoputri's husband, a pilot in the Indonesian airforce, was killed during President Sukarno's military campaign to wrest Netherlands New Guinea from the Dutch in 1961–62.

Sukarno acquired the title 'Great Son of West Irian' among Indonesians,[3] and was the subject of many apocryphal narratives at East Awin. Several older people claimed they had viewed a photograph showing Sukarno with his baton standing poised before a map of Netherlands New Guinea. The photograph's caption in Indonesian read that Netherlands New Guinea had been 'entrusted' to Sukarno. Contained in the word '*titip*' or 'entrust' is the meaning of temporary custodianship. One elderly Muyu man explained that if Megawati granted independence to West Papua, she would be rewarded with powers to govern the rest of Indonesia. He explained: 'Of course Megawati's party will be chosen by West Papua. She will see to her father's promise. She will know about the eagle.' It was said that the garuda eagle—the official seal of the Indonesian government—was native to West Papua, but only certain people could see it. In one such mythical account, Sukarno, who it was believed had been interned at Boven Digoel (Netherlands new Guinea), met with one of these people to request permission to borrow the eagle for 30 years.[4] The request was granted, and in 1949 Indonesia became independent from the Dutch under the leadership of Sukarno—who broke his promise by not returning the eagle to the West Papuan people. Therein lies Indonesia's success: the garuda gives information to Indonesia about what must be done to achieve victory. Removal of the eagle's image left West Papua vulnerable to Indonesia's annexation and continued colonisation. The tactic doubles back: West Papua's power is borrowed by Sukarno to defeat the Dutch, and then used by Indonesia to colonise West Papua.

Like the apocryphal stories about Sukarno, song lyrics also recalled and made history. West Papuans describe themselves as song-makers, and song-making as an enduring cultural tradition and expression of West Papuan humanity. Arnold Ap's ditty was famous among West Papuans: 'I sing to live, singing is a sign of life. If I am not singing it means I am already dead.' The state's suspicion of song-making was manifest in the murder of Ap in 1984. Inside Irian Jaya, song-makers deployed metaphor to disguise meaning. Outside, liberated song-makers have composed unambiguous lyrics that catalogue events and practices of colonisation such as PEPERA 1969, which saw West Papuan 'delegates' vote in favour of incorporation into the Indonesian state. Alex Hanueby's song 'Changes in 1969' depicts the year as a revolutionary juncture for West Papuan people. Arranged in Tok Pisin, the lingua franca of Papua New Guinea, Hanueby had in mind a Papua New Guinean audience when he wrote this song at East Awin:

> In the past, in the land where the sun goes down
> You were a pleasant place where the cool breeze always blew
> Many birds of paradise made their song
> All kinds of flowers decorated your forest
> All the people were happy, moved around freely
> Betel nuts, sago and game were plentiful
> They had gold and silver
> People's lives were not too hard
> But in 1969 things changed
> Enemies came and stole your people's land
> Destroyed their rights ... now they are poor
> In your country.

Children and adults learned of colonising practices via lyrics like Jack Offide's song 'Port Numbay' below, composed at Blackwater settlement near Vanimo in 1984. Port Numbay is the local name for the capital, which has been variously named Jayapura, Sukarnopura, Kotabaru and Hollandia. Name changes in Irian Jaya make no reference to indigenous toponyms in use among local resident communities:[5]

> Do you know the capital of West Papua?
> Like a precious pearl in the evening
> A cool breeze blows on the Cyclops mountain peak
> From Yotefa Bay that is the city of Port Numbay, the capital of West Papua
> Your name truly glows in the human heart
> You are the words of our praise, I cherish you
> During the time of change you were called Kotabaru
> President Sukarno also called you Sukarnopura
> The Indonesian nation exalted you, city of Jayapura.

The colonial practice of naming was collectively understood as an effort to inculcate the Indonesians as liberators against the colonial Dutch. Spectacular mountain peaks and ranges were renamed to invoke Indonesian liberation. The Juliana peak of Dutch times became the Suharto peak, and Mount Juliana became Mandala mountain, named after Suharto's 1962 military command for the liberation of Netherlands New Guinea. The Nassau mountains became the Sudirman range after the Javanese guerrilla who led the 1945–49 armed struggle against the Dutch on Java. Mount Wilhelmina became Mount Trikora after Sukarno's campaign to liberate Netherlands New Guinea from Dutch control. Frederik Hendrik Island south of Merauke became Yos Sudarso Island after the Javanese commodore who led a doomed attack on a Dutch warship.

Public gatherings at East Awin provided opportunities for political songs and speeches that recalled history. I witnessed historical speeches at the tenth birthday party of Michael, sponsored by his maternal uncle in Amsterdam; the sixtieth birthday of Yohanes the Arfai veteran; the tenth anniversary of the Immanuel Protestant Church; a farewell celebration for repatriates in the Wamena Baptist Church; and many funerals. At these gatherings, a speaker would inevitably begin by apologising to guests for the austerity of the occasion caused by their circumstances as refugees living in the rainforest. It was explained that in their own place, the ceremony would have properly fitted the occasion. From here the speaker would describe how their situation as refugees had been compelled by the violent annexation of their homeland.

At East Awin, people read about history as well as speaking and singing it, and several historical texts circulated. Multiple copies of a 50-page manuscript titled 'Historical Data of West Papua from 1511–1998' passed among Muyu people who had received them from relatives in Irian Jaya. Supported by the Catholic Church, several refugee teachers conducted history classes for adults and students based on it. One teacher used the word 'public' or 'common' to describe the course's approach, claiming that the history they taught was commonly or collectively accepted, rather than from any West Papuan factional standpoint. The booklet cautioned against colonial versions of West Papuan history:

This data was arranged because a large segment of the Papuan population, especially West Papuans, do not yet know their history, and consequently are easily deceived and dominated by other nations or people from outside ... Current published history is completely subjective, which means that history has been totally engineered according to the interests of the colonisers. [We] have endeavoured to straighten out/correct history which has led the Papuan nation astray... it is extremely dangerous if Papuan people do not know the course of the history of the Papuan nation. Because other nations will distort the course of our history in order to annihilate Papuans and their rights until history becomes completely subjective ... History holds an important role in the development of a nation. One can look to the past, the present and the future ... History and politics are partners which cannot be separated, because politics without history is blind and history without politics is lame. (Foreword)

Reading material was loaned tentatively at East Awin as borrowers could not be routinely trusted to return an item, or return it intact. In spite of this, literature did circulate between households. Newsletters compiled by West Papuans living in the Netherlands were posted to East Awin by relatives. The literature contained photographs, cartoons, and reports from West Papuans inside and outside Irian Jaya, about current and historical political events. Outdated copies of newspapers published in Jayapura like *Tifa Irian* and *Cenderawasih Pos* educated readers about social and economic issues in the capital and districts. A limited amount of popular literature on 'the struggle' also circulated at East Awin. Non-English readers used the photographs in these books to identify various leaders and other people to me—as though it were their personal album or record of events. Such books included George Monbiot's *Poisoned arrows*, Nonie Sharp's *Rule of the sword*, Carmel Budiardjo and Liem Soei Liong's *West Papua: the obliteration of a people*, and Robin Osborne's *Indonesia's secret war*. Nonie Sharp spoke about the impact of her book, which: '... [had] touched the nerve of Papuan self-recognition ... Papuans passed around the book among themselves; it was read widely in Papua New Guinea'.[6] Among English readers, these books may have contributed to the standardisation of some narratives as readers read published versions of particular events. It is probable that published versions of historical events entered local narratives.

In an early interview with Luther—who became a key interlocutor—he pulled out a dog-eared copy of Budiardjo's book, and used the photographs to illustrate his life story. As his insights are critical to this chapter and the next, it is fitting to introduce Luther here. He received a degree in education from the Cenderawasih University in Jayapura. In the early 1980s, he was arrested on suspicion of providing financial support to OPM militants, and spent nine months in solitary confinement in a damp cell with a concrete floor. The experience contorted his body. At East Awin, years of deprivation further diminished his health, and he suffered chronic anaemia caused by malnutrition, as well as repeated bouts of malaria. Luther brought irregular and small amounts of cash into the household by carving tortoiseshell and kenari nut. Such fine work in poor light had strained his eyes irreparably. His wife Sofia purchased oil and flour to cook Chinese steamed buns called *bapauw*, and egg rolls made with cassava flour known as *lumpia*. She sold these in the Saturday afternoon and Wednesday morning markets at East Awin. When they could afford it, Luther and Sofia purchased bulk kerosene and decanted it for resale into 500ml plastic bottles. The bottles of blue fluid were displayed in a window frame in the wall of their house, visible from the main road.

Luther and Sofia had relatives elsewhere in PNG from whom they occasionally sought financial help, but none in the Netherlands like some other northerners at East Awin. Like most other refugees, they lived almost entirely from their garden of sweet potatoes, bananas and plantain, and greens. They had five children. Their first-born, named after the West Papuan musician Arnold Ap, died tragically like his namesake. The infant Arnold was suffering from malaria when Luther and Sofia first arrived at Vanimo. Intending to inject Arnold with quinine, a nurse had asked Luther in Tok Pisin whether his son had an empty stomach. Not understanding Tok Pisin, Luther misunderstood the question and answered 'no'. The infant was injected with quinine and later died, apparently from toxicity. Luther blamed himself for his son's death. In the naming of Luther and Sofia's last-born son Emmanuel Koreri, Luther's religious politic is implicit. Emmanuel means 'God with us', and Koreri refers to the Biak religious movement whose central Jesus figure is destined to return to this world bringing a golden age of peace and wellbeing.

In our conversations about history, it was Luther's account of Dutch rule that countered the benevolent accounts of other West Papuans. For Luther, handing over Netherlands New Guinea to a transitional administration governed by Indonesia in 1962 amounted to political betrayal. But Indonesia's revisionist history allying West Papuans with Indonesians against the Dutch, and repositioning Indonesia as liberators of West Papuans, was also offensive. Luther's family had mourned the departure of the Dutch, and Luther described the event as like the loss of one's father: 'as though our father had been ordered to leave'. Some Dutch resisted, and were arrested and forcibly deported. According to Luther, 'Westerners were not permitted to stay for they had encouraged us to believe in independence.' It was because of this that:

> There was no feeling of enmity with the Dutch. There was no slaying in
> the Dutch time. Papuans felt profound sorrow and grief, even mourning
> at the sight of the Dutch leaving in ships in 1962–63. These emotions

are poignant. People still recall the names of the Dutch ships. Dutch citizens were repatriated by Indonesia, followed by Indo-European people. (Luther)

A peer of Arnold Ap's, Luther remembered a song composed by Ap in 1980–81 which used the metaphor of an orphan—an archetype of utter destitution in Indonesian popular culture. Written in the Biak language, Luther used Ap's own paraphrasing of the song 'Orphan Child' during a rehearsal:

> West Papuan people were like infants. What was needed or asked for was given. Upon coming of age and experiencing the abandonment of their [Dutch] parents, the infant became an orphan. The child remained an orphan despite its new Indonesian parentage. Indonesia is not a benevolent parent. The child must face life's hardships alone, without parents. It has no homeland.

The family trope implies obligation and moral responsibility. The 'naturalness' of the Dutch parent manifest in the expression of unselfish love contrasts Indonesia as a neglectful adoptive parent. In spite of adoption, the child's condition remains pitifully homeless. Yet the obligation of the first parent is not ignored either. During 1998 when a referendum for East Timor was being mooted, Luther stressed to me that the Dutch like Portugal must be responsible. He said: 'Now the Dutch must be responsible. Although Indonesia may grant independence [to West Papua], the Dutch must be present. Not like Portugal's withdrawal from East Timor. The Dutch have a role to play. Like a parent they must be responsible.'

Extending the family trope further, Luther claimed the Dutch had behaved towards West Papuans not as equal adults, but as children in relation to their adult selves. It was a racially based, hierarchical distinction that saw West Papuans treated differently from other peoples of the Empire.

> The Dutch differentiated themselves from Papuans. Restaurants were set aside for Dutch and Indo [mixed Indonesian–Dutch] people. Primary and secondary schools were set aside. Church times were differentiated. Dutch attended church services in the afternoon and evenings, Papuans in the morning. Papuans knew for themselves they were not Dutch people, it became custom for Papuans to attend morning church. In the cinema, Dutch time meant Papuans could not attend. There were buses for Papuans, buses for the Dutch. During this time, the Protestant missions employed Ambonese and the Roman Catholics employed Kai people from Maluku as teachers, missionary assistants and lay preachers. Kai people were labelled as Java's golden or favourite child: they were considered civilised and cultured.

Luther used the Indonesian school reader *Kota emas* (*The city of gold*) to speak about these relations. He read it as a subtle critique of Dutch colonial rule. The book's author Isaak Samuel Kijne was a Dutch missionary and teacher from the Utrecht Missionary Society. In 1958, Kijne published a songbook titled *The golden flute* which contained the song 'Hai Tanahku Papua',chosen as the West Papuan national anthem in 1961. Along with other Dutch texts, Kijne's books were confiscated by the Indonesian administration in 1962. As a child, Luther had 'watched with my own eyes, my teacher gather the Dutch books from the filing cupboard and take them outside and set them alight.' Retrospectively, Luther understood that: 'Kijne disguised our political struggle as a children's story. It was presented as a mere tale and did not feel political. The meaning ran much deeper though.' Both of Kijne's texts were reprinted in the Netherlands, and copies sent to East Awin. Luther characterised *The city of gold* as an historical and religious parable about unequal relations between West Papuans and Dutch, Indo and Moluccan people in the period of the 1940s and 1950s. The book elaborates on inequality between Dutch and Papuans in a period leading up to self-determination. The story centres on a friendship and its dissolution, between a Papuan boy named Tom and his Dutch friend Regina. In the course of Regina's abandonment of Tom, she reflects on her treatment of him: '[Tom] has never used coarse words to me. Never used nasty words. And I am the one who always wants to play the gentleman or the lady [while] he is left to play the slave or houseboy.' Without Tom, Regina sets out on her own journey to the so-called city of gold, which is interpreted variously in terms of a metaphorical field of heaven, liberation and freedom. Regina then returns to fetch Tom as she realises that she cannot make the journey on her own, for her salvation is dependent on her relationship with him. Luther's interpretation is that Dutch fate is tied up with their abandonment of Netherlands New Guinea.

To Luther's dismay, published histories of Indonesia and national museum dioramas represent Indonesia as liberating West Papua from the colonial Dutch. Even the meaning of 'Irian' was fabricated, for it was Indonesia that corrupted it into the acronym for: 'Pro-Indonesian Republic, anti-Netherlands'. The notion of liberation is represented figuratively in the West Irian Freedom Statue in front of the Treasury Building in Jakarta. It depicts a West Papuan man bared to the waist, his trouser-legs rolled up to display the broken chains of his leg irons. His hair is tousled, his arms are flung wide as though victorious, and his open mouth proclaims freedom loudly. This is the enslaved West Papuan relinquishing his Dutch shackles. Also in Jakarta, the Satriamandala Museum contains 74 dioramas representing events surrounding the battle for independence, and the role of the nationalist movement and civilian population in the lead up to it. Netherlands New Guinea is represented as pro-Indonesian. Diorama number 39 titled 'Irianese resistance March 14, 1948' depicts an attack on a Dutch barracks by West Papuans. Diorama number 56 is titled 'Mandala Command for the

Liberation of Irian January 2, 1962.' While some West Papuans did support Indonesia against the Dutch in the 1940s and early 1960s, and some also shifted their allegiance away from Indonesia in this period, the Indonesian version of West Papuan people as categorically anti-Netherlands is a convenient fiction.

In 1998, an Indonesian government inquiry reported on factors relating to the flag-raising incidences that had occurred across Irian Jaya in July of that year.[7] The inquiry concluded that the history of Irian Jaya ought to be taught, particularly the matter of Irianese national patriots who were allies of Indonesia during the TRIKORA (an Indonesian acronym for People's Triple Command for the Liberation of West Irian) campaign to liberate Irian Jaya. Otherwise, young Irianese would remain ignorant about the history of Irianese patriots of the Indonesian state in national battles of liberation in 1945–49 and 1962–63. The state's revisionist project recovers historical precedence of pro-Indonesian sentiment, identifying Irianese as patriots and founding members of the republic. But West Papuan narratives that elaborate preparation by the Dutch towards a West Papuan nation-state subvert the state's popular version that Indonesia liberated Irian Jaya from the Dutch.

Undoubtedly, the TRIKORA action on 19 December was inspired by the West New Guinea Council (22 out of 28 seats held by Papuans) vote on 1 December 1961 to rename Netherlands New Guinea as West Papua, adopt 'Hai Tanahku Papua' as the national anthem and promote the Morning Star flag as the national flag. The anthem and flag raised the President's ire. Part of his TRIKORA declaration speech reads:

> But now at present in West Irian, the Dutch set up a 'state of Papua', they fly the 'flag of that state of Papua', they create a 'Papua anthem'. What must we here do? There is nothing else to do, we here must act. Act. And that is why I now give a Command to the entire Indonesian people. And what is my Command? Listen! My Command positively and clearly is: Frustrate, come now, all you people of Indonesia, defeat the setting up of that 'state of Papua'! What is my further Command? Come now, all you people of Indonesia, unfurl the Honoured Red White Flag in West Irian! I give this Command positively and clearly. Defeat this 'state of Papua'! Unfurl the Red and White Flag in West Irian! Defeat it! Unfurl our flag! Be prepared, general mobilisation is coming! General mobilisation which will involve the whole of the people of Indonesia in order to liberate West Irian completely from the stranglehold of Dutch imperialism.[8]

In the West Papuan reckoning, they were in a nascent state at the time of Indonesian annexation. Time and time again at East Awin I heard versions of the following imminence narrative:

> The state paraphernalia was complete. Flag, anthem, constitution, symbol of state and basis or constitution. The Dutch left behind the national anthem and flag, a foundation upon which we have struggled. The West Papuan flag had flown alongside the Dutch one. The Parliament had been configured. All that remained was international recognition. We had almost attained independence only to have it thieved. Indonesian dismantled and dispersed the Cabinet. We were already independent, and our independence was stolen in the light of day. Now we are waiting for our nationhood to be returned. Independence is the right of every nation. Why did Indonesia seize West Papua? Indonesia is thief, plunderer and agitator.

The West Papuan Morning Star flag is configured as 13 horizontal blue and white stripes with a white star at the centre of a single vertical red stripe. The 'morning star' known as *bintang kejora* in Indonesian, exists in Biak[9] and other local legend, as well as the Bible's New Testament where it is used figuratively to mention Christ. Dutch preparation of West Papua towards nationhood is recalled in the flag's colour. At East Awin, an artist called Solomon loaned me a short manuscript written by West Papuan Nicholas Jouwe titled '30 years of the West Papuan national flag'. Jouwe writes that West Papuan appropriation of the red, white and blue colours of the Dutch flag was done out of: 'eternal gratitude from our nation to the Dutch Empire' and 'because the Dutch government voluntarily gave the unconditional opportunity to the West Papuan population to determine the date of independence for the homeland and nation'. Solomon read the colours as signs. When Indonesia attained independence from the Dutch they retained the red representing struggle, and the white for purity, but discarded blue representing peace or compromise. If the Indonesian flag had retained the blue they might have accommodated the demands of the West Papuan people.

Misrepresentation of 'liberation' is also rehearsed in speeches that commemorate the first battle of Arfai on 28 July 1965 where West Papuan members of a former Dutch battalion fought against Indonesian soldiers. Yohanes, an Arfai veteran, described this battle as the first activity of West Papuan resistance to Indonesia. Captured by the Indonesians after Arfai, Yohanes was 're-educated' before being co-opted into the Indonesian army where he proceeded to stage his own small-scale sabotage tactics. According to Yohanes, Indonesia disbanded his battalion of Dutch-trained West Papuans because a national army is a potent symbol of nation, and the Papuan Battalion anticipated this state. Battalion soldiers retaliated by launching an attack on an Indonesian base with machetes, axes, knives and guns. These weapons were remnants from World War II dropped by the United States air force for West Papuans to use against the Japanese. The battle of Arfai inspired events of resistance in other parts of West

Papua. In response, Indonesian campaigns were orchestrated to eliminate resistance and activists, namely the OPM.

According to Yohanes, between 1963 and 1965, Indonesian soldiers shot or beat West Papuan soldiers and civilians without trial. Use of the word 'West Papua' was a criminal offence. West Papuan flags in government offices were lowered, soaked with kerosene, and burned. House to house searches were conducted, and flags and Kijne's songbook containing the national anthem were confiscated. 'Indonesian soldier' should not be conceived as a monolithic category though, for different military units sustain competing interests that have led to physical clashes.[10] But it should be said that West Papuans at East Awin invariably used 'Indonesian soldier' or 'ABRI' to label all military activity in Irian Jaya, indicating their experience of coherent Indonesian military power against West Papuan resistance. International observers like Amnesty International have identified a pattern of arrest and detention of West Papuans by the Indonesian state. First, where a person is suspected of OPM involvement, arrest, interrogation and detention without trial occurs. Second, people previously detained and released are likely to be detained again. Third, after detention and release, people are required to report to the police two or three times per week. Fourth, when incidents occur, en masse arrests are carried out. Fifth, relatives of suspects are detained, and sixth, detainees are recruited as spies for the state.[11]

It was not until 1969 that Indonesia's occupation was internationally recognised with the incorporation of Irian Jaya as its twenty-seventh province. West Papuans at East Awin upheld the 1969 Act of Free Choice as the pre-eminent proof of Indonesian deceit. The narratives relating to PEPERA are collective. Simply mentioning '1969' to the West Papuans I talked to would provoke an historical monologue. It was to West Papuans at East Awin what '9:11' is to Americans, in the sense that both are historical conjunctures. Even the gestures accompanying a monologue about 1969 are standardised, usually deploying an imaginary pistol pointed to the head. The 1969 monologues usually catalogue the deceptive elements of PEPERA: instead of 'one person one vote' as originally agreed upon by the UN, Indonesia arranged '1000 represented by one'; old men who could not read or write were chosen; delegates were not permitted to speak to people outside; soldiers guarded the entrance and delegates were accompanied wherever they went; delegates were fed well and given gifts of teapots, plates, Sanyo radios, bicycles and Honda motorcycles; and some were given Javanese women and taken to Jakarta where they stayed in fancy hotels. Shaking his head at their naivety in the face of such deception, Yohanes said: 'They thought their life would be like that under Indonesia.' On voting day, voters were given rice and tinned fish distributed by the neighbourhood association and their inked thumbs were 'guided' by Indonesian electoral officers. Planes then scattered thousands of pamphlets from the sky that said: 'We the people of West Papua, with this, become as one with the Indonesian Republic.' 'But afterward,' explained Johanes, 'life returned to the way it had been before. In retrospect we realised that we had sold ourselves, sold our land.'

The 1969 monologues lay PEPERA's implementation bare: tactical selection, concealment, bribery and seduction by objects associated with pleasure. In the period of the late 1960s, imported items like Sanyo radios and Honda motorbikes were both extremely expensive, and rarely owned by West Papuans. These were the first gifts in a series of deceptions that the Indonesian state, and migrants, deployed in order to gain power and land. West Papuans at East Awin recalled the event of PEPERA as fraudulent, whereas Jakarta recalls it as unanimous. After 1969, West Papuans were subject to various colonisation policies. In a speech recorded during an Arfai commemorative ceremony at Blackwater camp at Vanimo in 1987, the Indonesian state's penetration of West Papua was described in terms of the strangling banyan tree:

> The banyan tree is Indonesia's national symbol. For West Papuans, this tree harbours tutelary spirits, it is a place of Satan. It is a colonising vine which strangles the tree of attachment, dominating the environment. The eagle is another symbol of state. It is predator and hunter, seizing prey ruthlessly. Yes, these two symbols represent the Indonesian style of governmentation. Why are black-skinned West Papuans not protected by the banyan tree? Why are our rights not the same as other Indonesians from Java, Sulawesi, Sumatra? The banyan tree is not a place of sanctuary but the reverse, a sign of murder, violation of basic human rights, and the dignity of the Papuan people. The Indonesian state is the same as the banyan tree in its natural environment: strangling other plants nearby. The main task of the revolution is to destroy the banyan tree down to its very roots.

(Transcribed from Luther's tape.)

The colonising banyan tree is a striking analogy. According to West Papuan cosmology, the banyan tree is a place of evil. (It is difficult to ascertain whether this meaning pre-dates its incorporation as Suharto's Golkar Party symbol.) The Vanimo speech inverts the symbol of the former ruling party, claiming that it was under the tree's guise of supposed protection during Golkar rule that West Papuans have experienced greatest vulnerability. The speech recasts the banyan tree not as a benign sign of protection or salvation, but one of danger and neglect.

Indonesia's annexation has allowed massive resource extraction. West Papuans at East Awin described the world as living on their wealth, particularly the Grasberg gold and copper mine complex of Freeport-Indonesia, a subsidiary of the New Orleans-based mining corporation Freeport McMoRan. West Papua constitutes Java's kitchen: it feeds the rest of Indonesia. It is also the destination for Indonesian transmigrants. West Papuans characterise their homeland as a Garden of Eden, contrasting Java as a place of beggars where people sleep under bridges. Java is the antithesis of paradise. Transmigrants were viewed as slowly appropriating coastal land and spreading back into the interior, their habit modelling the banyan tree.

The spread of transmigrants was not quite so slow. In 1984, the Indonesian government's transmigration program projected an increase to approximately 138,000 families or 700,000 persons for the 1985–89 period.[12] Considering that 3000 hectares would be required for every 500 people, between 1.5 to 3.2 million hectares needed to be alienated.[13] Of 39 proposed sites, 12 lay within 30 kilometres of the border.[14] The rumoured arrival of hundreds of thousands of migrants from Indonesia, and the necessary appropriation of land, fed into the escalation of resistance in 1983–84. The International Court of Justice reported that West Papuan refugees claimed the Indonesian state's forced acquisition of their land to be a major reason for their resistance to Indonesia rule and struggle for independence.[15] However, by 1987 less than 3600 households or 3 per cent of the original target had been resettled in Irian Jaya due to cutbacks in the national budget, conflicts with indigenous landowners over matters of compensation and criticism of the potential demographic, social and economic impacts.[16]

Transmigration is not just about relocation of poor farmers. Transmigration policy also produces a category of local transmigrants called *translokal*. From 1976, where disputes occurred over land rights caused by transmigration, local people were compensated for the appropriation of their land by being incorporated into transmigration schemes as *translokal*. Under this program, 10 per cent of settlers were to come from the local population.[17] The settlement of retired soldiers on transmigration sites is public knowledge and the subject of diorama number 70 titled 'ABRI transmigrants outside Java' in the national military Satriamandala Museum in Jakarta.[18] According to West Papuans, the colonising project of transmigration disguises retired soldiers as farmers to act as agents for the state's business interests.

According to Luther, Dutch and Indonesian approaches to the management of natural resources were worlds apart. Indonesia alienated land and extracted wealth for its own interests, whereas the Dutch employed West Papuans, instructing them how to extract resources and look for things of value. A common proverb describes 'impoverished West Papuans walking above glorious riches'. In other words, the location of mineral wealth below the ground renders it inaccessible to West Papuan landholders. Indonesian practices of extraction and appropriation cause eviction and marginalisation of West Papuans. West Papuans sell their produce on the roadside where passing vehicles stir the dust, while migrants sell theirs in undercover marketplaces. Migrants fish from platforms and docks that they install, while West Papuans catch a few fish on the edges of these platforms. Even if they cast lines or nets far out to sea the catch will be small. Contrasting the situation of West Papuans with their neighbours, Luther explained:

> Our rights are not paid any due. We are called citizens but our rights are not the same as Indonesians. The banks discriminate against us, the requirements are so great, we feel we cannot even try. All sorts of letters and documents are required for even minor matters. In the garden, the village, the town and the state we are considered without rights. Here [PNG], indigenous people have full land rights. There [Irian Jaya], indigenous people are threatened at gunpoint and our land is state property.

He categorised West Papuans as second-class citizen in the eyes of the migrant and the state, mocking Indonesian citizenship as a veneer.

Ethnocide is the most extreme form of colonisation. Nurse Mientje spoke of her own experience working in hospitals in Irian Jaya. She analysed relations between Indonesian hospital staff and local patients in racial terms. She classified the following practices as 'indirect killing': intentional medical neglect, poisoning, and sterilisation. Mientje used the Indonesian word *halus* meaning 'concealed' to describe an act of killing antithetical to the sort of killing carried out in front of onlookers in daylight. (The West Papuan sorcerer figure known as *swanggi* carries out sinister killings that are concealed in this way.) Mientje said that medical treatment could exacerbate a West Papuan patient's condition. People even joked: 'if you want to die, go to hospital'. According to Mientje, Indonesian hospital staff differentiated between Indonesian and West Papuan patients. Seriously sick West Papuans could be denied immediate treatment, and denied proper examination. If a blood transfusion were required, no priority would be given to match the blood type or to summon relatives. At East Awin, deliberate poisoning was also anticipated. In a public meeting, I heard Yohanes warn that West Papuans from Merauke visiting refugee relatives were bringing sachets of cooking spices and monosodium glutomate for resale in the East Awin market. Yohanes said he had interrogated one visitor: 'Mama, brought this from there did you? Bought it from a small kiosk or shop or was it 'given' to you?'

Like poisoning, family planning was understood in terms of a rubric of elimination. In people's minds, it was related to sterilisation, and was viewed as a state program to systematically and covertly restrict West Papuan population growth. Some refugees told me their relatives had advised them to procreate in PNG, because sterilisation was taking place 'inside'. The rumour among some West Papuans that 'family planning kills' has been analysed in terms of three intimately connected realms: birth control methods that are physically invasive, historical memory of state violence and intimation or the potential of violence 'at an everyday level' in the present.[19]

The mention of family planning at East Awin, like the mention of 'TRIKORA' or '1969' or '*koteka* campaign' or 'Arnold Ap' or 'transmigration' or 'Freeport', elicit historical monologues about West Papuan experiences of Indonesian colonisation. Some theological scholars in West Papua have labelled the effect of these experiences as *memoria passionis* or collective 'memories of suffering'. This construct has circulated in public discourse in Irian Jaya since 1999, and draws on the earlier work of Johanes Baptist Metz.[20] Metz theorised *memoria passionis* to be manifest in a political consciousness and political action in the memory of people's suffering. The substance of *memoria passionis* is said to be inscribed in social memory, and flows incisively and clearly from the mouths of ordinary people:

> If we travel without prejudice to the remote places of Papua—Wamena, Paniai, the Jayawijaya Highlands, the Star Mountains, Mindiptana, Timika, Arso, Mamberamo—we will undoubtedly hear stories of suffering from the mouths of ordinary people. Their memories are clear and sharp, they have taken note of these things: 'In this river our father was murdered; on that mountain slope there used to be some villages. In this river our father was murdered; on the slope of that mountain there were many villages which were destroyed by ABRI; on that open field, our old men were forced to burn their *koteka* because they were considered primitive; in the past that mountain was ours, now people have destroyed our mother; before we easily hunted animals in the forest but now we are not permitted to enter and it is said the company is protected by state law; our children cannot advance because there are too few teachers in the school; medicine is too expensive.'[21]

These individual and collective memories of suffering since the period of Indonesian colonisation are said to drive a process of nationalism carefully labelled 'the idea of a New Papua':

> … here it needs to be understood that the idea of a New Papua like the case of an independent Papua, was born in the life experience of a group. It has not fallen from the sky. It is born: a) out of historical experience: the event of integration with the Republic of Indonesia which was forced upon Papuans by Indonesians began in the beginning of the 1960s while they were preparing to form a free and sovereign West Papua; b) interaction with Indonesian people, both government officials and business, who in the experience and understanding of the [West Papuan] people only come to seize the rights of Papuans and destroy them in the name of development; and c) the idea of a New Papua in the same manner as has been clarified above is not separate from *memoria passionis*: the

> experience of suffering of Papuans, both individually and collectively connected with the violation of human rights in the form of murder that has occurred for more than thirty years [and] has not ever been discharged/settled thoroughly.[22]

State-sponsored violence that is directed at West Papuans as a category can result in the creation of boundaries of a 'moral community', and 'canonisation' of the Other as inhuman.[23] The risk of canonisation is that one nationalism can become the racist inversion of another, because processes of nationalism and racism are forms of categorical thought; 'parallel constructions capable of interpermutation'.[24] In the context of West Papua, the idea of inversion focuses attention on the fate of Indonesians in the event of *merdeka*. The caution is sobering, for the narratives in this chapter appear to canonise the inhumanity of the category 'Indonesia'. Mote and Rutherford's analysis of primordialism extends further the idea of one nationalism becoming an inversion of the other, and the prospect of anti-migrant actions among West Papuans.[25] The authors call into question the idea that West Papuan antagonism towards Indonesian migrants is grounded in primordialism, or that West Papuanness is an assumed essence in opposition to 'arrivals' or migrants. Rather, they interrogate the state's actions through its soldiers and officials, to be provocative. They make the salient point that what appears like primordial violence in an incident may not have begun as primordial violence. But neither do they shy away from the prospect of primordial violence: 'Expectations concerning the "repressed passions" of others can work in explosive ways to orient action. It is not necessarily the given-ness of ethnic identities that leads to the spread of terror; it is the sudden emergence into view of feared categories of personhood that can lead people to suddenly recognise a neighbour as a potential threat.'[26]

Rosenau's concept of 'event cascades' explains the timing and location of ethnic conflict, shifting us still further from primordialist interpretation. He uses the metaphor of cascade to analyse conflict in a world that is multicentric, and where sequences of actions generate other events that spread. Events can 'reverberate[d] outward and upward, through other cascades of events.'[27] The events and campaigns orchestrated by the state in this chapter can be contextualised against the activities that precede and succeed them. Each incident and campaign generates other incidences and interpretations at the local level. Appadurai reads Rosenau's cascades as macro-events and processes that link global to micropolitics.[28] A macro or large-scale interaction within a nation-state might be invigorated by another event elsewhere, and then 'cascade through the complexities of regional, local, and neighborhood politics until they energise local issues and implode into various forms of violence.'[29] So transmigration, family planning, the *koteka* campaign and Ap's death constitute macro events and processes that produce ripples and pressures that become folded into local politics.

The violent death of Arnold Ap is integral to the repertoire of a West Papuan *memoria passionis* rehearsed in this chapter. Recognition of collective suffering under Indonesia inspired Ap to take cultural difference as the conscious object of his performance project. His boundary-making work caused him to be targeted by the state, and resulted in the incorporation of his violent death into *memoria passionis*. For northerner West Papuans at East Awin, Ap's suffering remains a potent memory. For Luther and Sofia, the memory of Ap's suffering lies at the very heart of their intention to hold out in exile.

ENDNOTES

1 Mote and Rutherford, p. 118.

2 Mote and Rutherford, p. 121.

3 Herb Feith, 'Indonesia's political symbols and their wielders', *World Politics Australia*, 1963, 16, p. 83.

4 Sukarno was exiled not to Boven Digul but to Flores and later Bengkoeloe in Sumatra. See T. Shiraishi, 'The phantom world of Digoel', *Indonesia*, 61, 1996, pp. 93–118; R. Mrazek, 'Sjahrir at Boven Digul: reflections on exile in the Dutch East Indies', In D. S. Lev and R. McVey (eds) *Making Indonesia*, Cornell University Press, Ithaca, 1996, pp. 41–65.

5 Chris Ballard, 'Blanks in the writing: possible histories for West New Guinea', *Journal of Pacific History*, 34, 2, 1999, pp. 149–55.

6 Nonie Sharp, *The Morning Star in Papua Barat*, Arena Publications, North Carlton, Australia, 1994, p. xv.

7 'There is no Irian Jaya history, history books asked to be revised', *Republika Online*, 25 August 1998.

8 Sukarno, 'The People's Command for the Liberation of West Irian', Department of Information, Republic of Indonesia, Special issue no. 82, 19 December 1961, *Papuaweb*, (http://www.papuaweb.org/goi/pidato/1961-12-jogyakarta.html).

9 George Aditjondro, 'Mengenang perjuangan Tom Wanggai: dengan bendera, atau apa?', *Tabloid Jubi*, 16, 29, 2000 (also at http://groups.yahoo.com./group/irianjaya/message/1485 (15 June 2008)).

10 Chris Ballard, 'The signature of terror: violence, memory and landscape at Freeport', in Meredith Wilson and Bruno David (eds), *Inscribed landscapes: the archaeology of rock-art, place and identity*, University of Hawaii Press, Honolulu, 2002, pp. 13–26.

11 Smith, pp. 311–14.

12 Manning and Rumbiak, *Economic development, migrant labour and indigenous welfare in Irian Jaya 1970–84*, Pacific Research Monograph no. 20, The Australian National University National Centre for Development Studies, Canberra, 1989, p. 46.

13 Peter Hastings, 'Prospects: 'a state of mind'', in R. J. May (ed.), *Between two nations: the Indonesia–Papua New Guinea border and West Papuan nationalism*, Robert Brown and Associates, Bathurst, 1986, p. 229.

14 Beverley Blaskett, 'Papua New Guinea–Indonesia relations: a new perspective on the border conflict', PhD thesis, The Australian National University, 1989, p. 163.

15 International Commission of Jurists, *Status of border crossers from Irian Jaya to Papua New Guinea*, Australian Section of International Commission of Jurists, Sydney, 1986.

16 Manning and Rumbiak, p. 48.

17 Blaskett, p. 165.

18 ABRI, *Museum ABRI Satriamandala buku panduan*, Angkata Bersenjata Republik Indonesia Pusat Sejarah dan Tradisi ABRI, Jakarta, 1997, pp. 109–110.

[19] Leslie Butt, 'Women and the perils of reproductive choice in Irian Jaya, Indonesia', in H. Lansdowne and M. Dobell (eds), *Women, culture and development in the Pacific*, Centre for Asia-Pacific Initiatives, Victoria, British Columbia, 2001, pp.65–73.

[20] J. B. Metz, *Faith in history and society: toward a practical, fundamental theology*, Burns and Oates, London, 1980.

[21] J. Budi Hernawan and Theo P. A. Van den Broek, Dialog nasional Papua sebuah kisah 'Memoria Passionis', Sekratariat Keadilan dan Perdamaian Keuskupan Jayapura. Jayapura March 1999, p. 3 (also at http://hampapua.org/skp/skp01/smp-04i.pdf (15 June 2008).

[22] Benny Giay, 'Menuju Papua Baru: Beberapa pokok pikiran sekitar emansipasi Orang Papua', Waena, Jayapura/Port Numbay, Deiyai/Els-ham Papua, p. 31.

[23] Malkki, p. 244.

[24] Malkki, p. 257; Anderson, p. 136.

[25] Mote and Rutherford.

[26] Mote and Rutherford, p. 124.

[27] Rosenau in Appadurai, p. 151.

[28] Rosenau in Appadurai, pp. 152–3.

[29] Appadurai, p. 164.

Chapter 2

Culture as the conscious object of performance

I stumbled across Arnold Ap in Benedict Anderson's book *Imagined communities* while reading for an undergraduate course in nationalism. Anderson wrote that the link between Ap's occupation as curator at the Cenderawasih University Museum in Jayapura and his 'assassination' was not accidental: 'for museums, and the museumising imagination, are both profoundly political'.[1] In 1997, 13 years after Ap's death, I visited the Cenderawasih Museum. It was in a parlous state. Walls were discoloured with mildew, and timber artefacts were so riddled with borers that unswept tailings lay piled beneath displays. The museum consisted of four galleries of ethnology and natural history. In the first gallery, various tools of war such as shields, spears and protective body vests filled the space. Being indigenous or 'Irianese' was essentialised in terms of warrior imagery. The third gallery celebrated another archetype: that of the Irianese wood carver. It was lined with exquisite Asmat artefacts, one of Jakarta's most lucrative craft exports. The second and fourth galleries exhibited items that added Irianese components to an Indonesian archipelago sequence: canoes, objects of brideprice, currency, Chinese porcelain, and cooking implements and pots. There were also two collections of photographs: one from Merauke in 1912 contributed by the Natural History Museum of America, and the other a Dutch collection from 1956.

At the time of my visit, the guide was a man of Lombok origin, an island to the east of Bali. I tried to engage him in a conversation about indigeneity by posing a question about the absence of West Papuan curators and museum staff. His answer contested my assumption that indigeneity ought to be positively discriminated. 'West Papuan-ness does not assume knowledge', he defended. 'So', I ventured, 'are there trained West Papuan curators working in museums elsewhere in Indonesia?' He appeared annoyed and it seemed pointless to continue, so I moved into the next gallery. The museum was deserted except for one other visitor, a big-haired man from Biak. In the second gallery he and I followed each other from one glass cabinet to the next without speaking.

Two weeks later I flew to Wamena in the highlands of Irian Jaya, and booked into a church guesthouse. By chance on a windswept breezeway between the bedrooms and amenities block, I ran into the Biak visitor from the museum. In spite of the roaring highland winds that would have drowned out any speech, he answered my questions in a voice that was barely audible. His nervousness caused me to be concerned. Did he really imagine someone might be listening? After I revealed to him that I was planning a trip to PNG to do research among West Papuan refugees, he told me his name (Piet), and the names of several of his friends who were refugees in PNG. But he advised me not to write anything that he told me on paper: there should be no record of our exchange. Towards the end of the conversation, Piet pulled his wallet from his shirt pocket and showed me the photograph he had positioned behind the clear plastic window. I knew many men who carried pictures of Jesus Christ in their wallets but Piet carried a photograph of Arnold Ap. Like Luther, Piet had been a student peer of Ap's and had played in one of his performance troupes. He had not fled to Vanimo like so many others, but Ap's death had marked Piet. Almost a year later at East Awin, I extended Piet's greeting to the friends he had mentioned. They nodded vaguely, perhaps ambivalent about his success, for remaining in Jayapura had allowed Piet to rise to the rank of senior civil servant in the Indonesian administration.

Map 2. Irian Jaya and the border region of Papua New Guinea showing the location of Cenderawasih University (UNCEN), Jayapura, East Awin, and regions from where Ap recorded performance material.

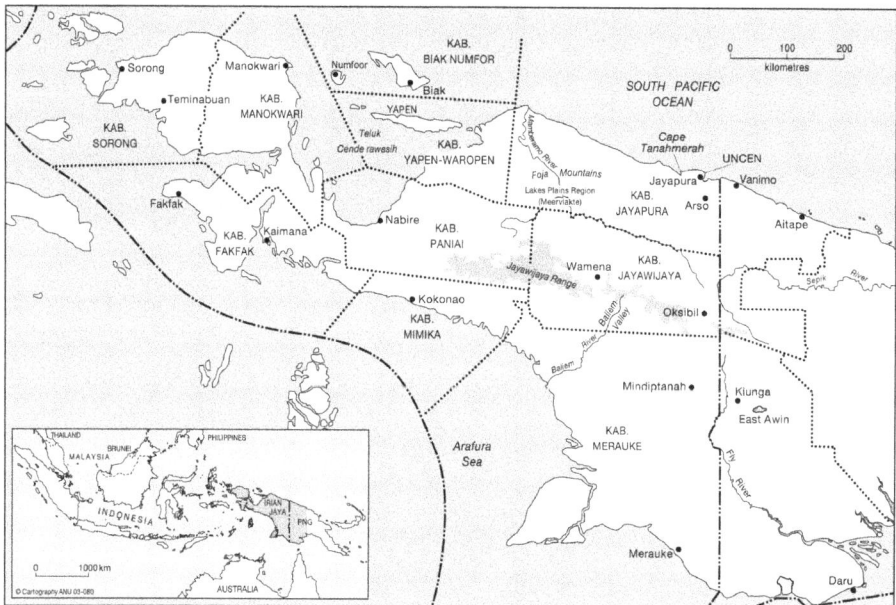

Map: Cartographic Services, Research School of Pacific and Asian Studies, College of Asia and the Pacific, The Australian National University.

The form of Ap's work, and how it resonated among West Papuans at East Awin, is the focus of this chapter. His biographical details are sourced from the spoken and written words of two of his peers: Luther and George Aditjondro. Luther was a member of Ap's group Mambesak. Aditjondro's book *Cahaya Bintang*

Kejora (*The radiance of the Morning Star*) contains several essays on Ap including: 'Indigenisation and Westernisation: the echo of Mambesak binding the cultural identity of the Cassowary Land' and 'The overlapping of individual and collective human rights in West Papua: taking as a starting point the case of Arnold Ap and Mambesak'. During Ap's curatorship, Aditjondro was Director of the Irian Jaya Development Information Service Centre which was located in the Cenderawasih Museum. Ap was an adviser to Aditjondro's organisation. His public identity was activated during the 1969 Act of Free Choice voting period when he led a demonstration with fellow Cenderawasih University students and was imprisoned at the Gunung Ifar prison outside Jayapura. Following his release, it was said that Ap made a conscious decision to engage West Papuan people in the preservation of their cultural identity, in spite of their existence within the Indonesian nation-state.[2]

Ap's movement can be taken as counter-ethnicity of sorts, and we can locate its emergence in Indonesian nationalist efforts to construct the ethnic category of 'Indonesian' and 'Indonesian national culture'. Appadurai's concept of 'culturalism' as the basis of mobilisation speaks to Ap's work. Appadurai characterises culturalist movements as tending to be counter-national, and involving 'deliberate, strategic, and populist mobilisation of cultural material'.[3] 'Culturalism' refers to a conscious mobilisation of cultural difference that is directed at nation-states.[4] Appadurai makes the point that where a nation-state is preoccupied with 'control, classification and surveillance' of its subjects, it can effect the creation or revitalisation of an ethnic category that was previously fluid or nascent.[5] The project of culturalism resonates with Ap's project which mobilised cultural performance (song, dance, music) to articulate a boundary of difference.[6] Writing, performing and exhibiting in the 1970s and 1980s in a dominated political environment, Ap's 'model of cultural shape'[7] that underpinned his practice rendered West Papuan cultural form localised and boundary-oriented. (More recent ideas of cultural forms as overlapping without boundaries, structures or regularities does not allow for this clear separation of entitities.[8])

In the late 1970s, Ap was appointed Curator of the Cenderawasih University Museum by Ignasius Suharno, the Director of the Institute of Anthropology. Funds were received from The John D. Rockefeller III Fund to establish a university museum, train a curator at the Bernice Bishop Museum in Hawai'i and purchase equipment and ethnographic collection items. Museum bequests were also received from the Papua and New Guinea Museum and Art Gallery. At the time, Ap was a performance artist: he sang, danced, played guitar, ukelele and *tifa*-drum and narrated satirical skits known as *mop*. He had intimate ties with customary leaders and artists and was a geography graduate from the Cenderawasih University.

Ap's museum was located within the Institute of Anthropology. The university had been established by a special presidential decree on 10 November 1962, 10 weeks after the UN Transitional Authority had taken over administrative responsibility from the Dutch, and six months before sovereignty was relinquished to Indonesia. Commentators claimed the Indonesian government hurried the establishment of a university to represent a dual symbol of the liberation of Netherlands New Guinea from Dutch colonialism, and Indonesia's reclamation of the eastern-most part of its archipelago.[9] A university would equalise Irian Jaya's status with the other provinces of Indonesia. It boasted several faculties including the Institute of Anthropology, intended as a research institution. The Institute's flagship publication was *Irian: Bulletin of West Irian* which was published from 1971 until 1993. Funds were received from the Asia Foundation, Jakarta, for research activity and to publish *Irian*. Linguists from the Summer Institute of Linguistics (SIL) co-edited the journal, and from 1973 produced a cooperative research program with the Institute. The bulletin's first editorial stated that *Irian*'s principal function was not as an academic journal, but to serve the people of West Irian and publish research findings relevant to government policy, particularly economic development.

In the 1970s, the Institute of Anthropology sponsored research into the impact of state and foreign enterprises on indigenous people—for example, the effectiveness of cooperatives initiated by the Catholic mission in the Asmat region, culture change and development in the Baliem Valley, the impact of Macassan immigrants on the economy of Greater Jayapura, and socio-economic surveys of the copra industry at Sorong and fishing industry at Jayapura. A university workshop report described local efforts to ground the subject and practice of university research in terms of the 'state directive of community service'.[10] At Cenderawasih University this was to be met through action research practice, village-based work experience, village education, provision of legal aid and co-operation with other non-government organisations. Research and teaching were to be grounded in matters relating to village life, re-settlement, transmigration areas and protection of natural resources. The function of research was to understand the community's 'issues' and build local problem-solving capacity to address the social, cultural and political issues emerging as a result of development.

This was the milieu in which Ap practised his curatorship. It has been said that the museum in the university functioned as the 'primary maker' of Irianese nationalism.[11] But others have proposed that the cultural performance movement on the edge of the museum, particularly the activities of Ap's performance troupe Mambesak, were more likely to inspire West Papuan nationalism among followers.[12] Mambesak's repertoire was restricted to songs and dances considered 'traditional', and originating from within West Papua. The bounded nature of the repertoire imagined a certain cultural congruity—an overarching cultural West Papuanness. Whereas the state's discourse of nationhood imagines different ethnicities as congruent parts of a unified Indonesian archipelago. Provinces are conceived as parts that form a unified national whole. The 'unified archipelago' concept is the basis of orthodox Indonesian museum practice where sequences of material culture items from different provinces of the archipelago are displayed.[13] Cultural items like folk stories, motifs, costumes and dances are arranged to form archipelago-wide sequences. This is evident in the second gallery of the museum, which displays canoes, objects of bride-price and cooking implements: items that can be replicated across the archipelago in sequential form. These sequences represent both the distinctiveness of an ethnic group, and its congruence as part of the archipelago.

Batik is one such cultural object that is said to manifest sequentially across the nation-state, including Irian Jaya. The Irian Jaya newspaper *Cenderawasih Post* reported on 8 July 1997 that the wife of Sultan Hamengkubuwono X of Jogjakarta visited transmigrants from her own 'sultanate' living in Irian Jaya. Known as Arso XI, this transmigration site is located near the Indonesian–PNG border. The Sultan's wife was welcomed by transmigrant children dancing Yospan, a popular dance synthesised from many local dances and represented as Irian Jaya's official provincial dance. Upon her appraisal of their dance performance, the children asked the Sultan's wife to give them a new *gamelan*, an ensemble of percussion instruments particular to Java and Bali. She agreed and then proceeded to advise them to produce batik using Irianese motifs that could become a national design. By doing so they would follow the lead of other transmigrants from Jogjakarta who produce Kalimantan motifs on batik. Batik using Irianese motifs comes to be represented as 'Irian batik', and Irian Jaya becomes incorporated into a regional cultural sequence of batik producers.

The tension between congruence and distinctiveness is also played out in the artistic display of small groups on cosmopolitan stages.[14] Hughes-Freeland's review of the 1989 London tour of a group of artists from the Asmat region of the south-east coast of Irian Jaya provides an example.[15] The Asmat group was organised by the Asmat Progress and Development Foundation, established by the speaker of the Indonesian House of Representatives in Jakarta. The Foundation's aim was to 'promote and preserve the existence of Asmat culture within the ethnic group in Indonesia', enabling them to 'participate in their national development without losing their identity and culture'.[16] Hailing from the Jakarta Arts Institute, the choreographer's job was to 'make' dances with various groups across the archipelago. At the London performance a public announcement informed the audience that Asmat dancers did not usually perform to an audience, and that the choreographed dance would comprise six Asmat rituals including initiation and spirit rites. But the fantasy of artistic display became unstuck, and the observer Hughes-Freeland said the London audience was disenchanted, and the performers were even less so:

> The most real moment of the event was after the audience had left, and the dancers gathered behind the walls of shields and *bis*-poles and sang a lament. 'They are homesick' said the organiser; but the sickness was more permanent than that, and the song spoke of more than any part of the staged show had done.[17]

The idea of preserving a local or regional culture within a national one is reflected in the metaphor *khasana* meaning 'storage area'. In an essay in the edited collection titled *Aspects and prospects of the cultural arts of Irian Jaya*, Ap used the metaphor of 'treasury' or storage area for valuable objects, to imagine a national culture as a container of regional cultural sequences:

> … clearly variegated arts of regional cultures need to be uncovered and cultivated and processed as well as developed in order to fill and enrich the national culture's treasury.[18]

Anthropologists have drawn attention to the way that regional diversity is honoured and valued by the Indonesian state as long as it remains at the level of display and performance, rather than belief or enactment.[19] Robinson expresses this eloquently: ' … the kinds of cultural differences which can be legitimately sustained are subjected to state-defined parameters of what kinds of cultural differences can be legitimately expressed'.[20] The orthodoxy of the 'unity in diversity' concept allowed Ap and his collaborator, composer Sam Kapissa, a certain liberty to represent West Papuan performance art and material culture as regional, so long as it was located alongside other regions and within the wider national culture. It provided justification for their own project, allowing a sense of 'alternative identity' to be sustained.[21] While Ap did not explicitly represent his viewpoint in relation to Indonesian cultural forms as intrusive, or West Papuan cultural identity as alternative, it was implicit in his practice and according to some of his peers was the subject of their private conversation with him.

Ap accompanied anthropologists on fieldwork trips, and used these opportunities to notate and record songs and dances, and document material culture such as carving, sculpture and pottery. He occasionally published this research.[22] In his essay 'Inventory of basic dance steps from Irian Jaya',[23] Ap detailed dance steps from four regions, and proposed that the foundation movements of every traditional dance were a response to the surrounding environment of that dance's location:

> … uncovering regional dance material which is still abundant in our region must be worked on with detail and care so that we don't disregard certain elements which constitute the character or identity of the dance

material mentioned. In order that we can account for each element which is presented we need to gather information or data from around the area of the region of origin of that dance material.[24]

Costumes made of local materials autochthonised the dance, allowing its origin to be traced to a locality. Imported materials were claimed to erase the identity of the dance.[25] Ap characterised the impact of the Indonesian media on local dance as 'polluting' and advocated that choreographers utilise traditional dance material:

> … it is still too early in Irian Jaya to busy ourselves with 'creative dance' because that type is suitable for regions that have already exhausted their regional dance material. We need to direct our attention to unearthing traditional dance material which is still abundant and preserve it so that it can then be worked on in 'new creations'.[26]

Ap and his peers choreographed the Yospan dance,[27] which was exhibited as one of several provincial icons in the Irian Jaya pavilion at the miniature cultural theme park Taman Mini, Jakarta, in the 1990s. In spite of its synthesis from several dances (Pancar, Yosim, Lemonipis and Balengan), the Yospan can be traced back to the local places of its constituent parts. Luther traced its origin as though its genealogies were constant:

> The Pancar dance is reckless. It reflects Biak's hot climate. It comprises sets of leaping or jumping movements called tuna fish and forward retreat repetitions called prawn. The dancer vigorously strikes his own buttocks with the heel making a sound like crashing of waves. The leaping movement in striking is like the exhilaration one feels running alongside breaking waves. The Yosim dance from Serui is slow and inviting. It is a firm stepping dance because Serui houses are close to the ground. It may have originated from Sarmi, taking its name from the Yosim mountain there. It is said that a student from Sarmi taught friends to dance Yosim while at school in Serui. The Lemonipis dance comes from Sarmi, Jayapura. It is characterised by rules and synchronised steps. Dancers hold hands and dance in a large group usually in a field, not in a house, circling a person beating the *tifa*-drum. The Balengan dance from Manokwari is more refined with little body movement. Steps are tread lightly because houses in this region are built high above swamps.

Ap's approach as curator, composer and choreographer was to preserve foundation elements from various localities, and also use these as the basis for innovation. Such local elements included composition structures, cadences, minor form, movements and gestures and language. (Mambesak recorded songs in thirty local languages.) These elements were used to 'Papuanise' foreign music from elsewhere in the archipelago and beyond. For example, hymns were commonly Papuanised by translating lyrics into regional languages, and utilising familiar composition structures and local instruments.[28] In the 1970s, Arnold Ap and Sam Kapissa complained that the European orientation of the liturgical music of the Christian Protestant Church was not 'rooted' in their own culture. In protest, they arranged religious songs in the languages of Biak, Windesi, Skou, Yali and Aitinyo, accompanied by accordion, *tifa*-drum, ukelele and guitar.[29] The trend toward Papuanising music in the Protestant Church in the north spread to Catholic congregations in the south.[30]

Photo 1. Yospan dancing accompanied by Mambesak musicians in front of the Governor's Office, Jayapura (Kapissa is the spectacled dancer facing the photographer, and Ap is second guitarist from right), c.1981.

Photo: Marthen Rumabar, previously published in 'Teaching performance art is like sharpening the blade of a knife', *The Asia Pacific Journal of Anthropology*, 5, 1, April 2004, pp. 1–14.

In 1974, Ap, Kapissa and their Biak peers formed a performance group called Manyori, meaning 'sacred bird indigenous to Biak-Numfoor'. Four years later they changed the name from Manyori to Mambesak. The name change is explained in terms of the symbolism of birds: *manyori* was a sacred bird native only to Biak-Numfor, whereas *mambesak* (bird of paradise) was revered throughout Irian Jaya.[31] Mambesak member Sawaki described the bird of paradise in analogous terms.[32] The bird of paradise, like any nation, includes varieties of different colour, size and movement. Like the various ethnic or tribal groups imagined as the West Papuan nation, the classification 'bird of paradise' comprises multiple species. The bird of paradise, too, has a history of appropriation and theft. The image of the island as bird-shaped has been commonplace since the Dutch period when the northwest peninsula was named 'Vogelkop' meaning 'bird's head'. There are further layers of symbolism in the mapping of Irian Jaya as the upper body of the bird-shaped island of New Guinea:

> The Island of Papua can be divided and compared with the body of a bird: Samarai to Port Moresby in Papua New Guinea is the bird's tail; Port Moresby to Nabire in West Papua is the bird's body; Nabire to Waropen is the bird's neck; Manokwari together with the Arfai mountain range is the bird's chignon; Lake Ayamaru is considered the bird's eye; Bintuni Bay in the Fak Fak region is the bird's lung and mouth/gullet; the mountain range in the middle is the bird's backbone; Yos Sudarso Island (Kimaam) and the estuary of the Digul River is the stomach and anus of the bird; the rivers on the island of Papua are the arteries; the dense forests are the bird's feathers.[33]

In renaming the group, members sought a regional translation of 'bird of paradise' that was already popular among West Papuans. The Biak '*mambesak*' was chosen because it became a household name following the televised performance of a '*mambesak* dance' at Taman Mini in Jakarta in April 1975.

The Mambesak group responded to Indonesian state efforts to manufacture provincial 'Irianese' performance. At provincial and national occasions, a mandatory folksong was usually represented by the Biak tune 'Apuse', a song of farewell composed in the 1930s by a teacher evangelist.[34] The prominence of folksongs like 'Apuse' at such occasions must have been jarring for Ap and Kapissa. Yet many West Papuans, perhaps reflecting Indonesian attitudes, were ambivalent about their own songs and dances: 'Melanesian songs were at that time only identified with village people and not popular among town dwellers of various origin and nationalities, even the Melanesians. Songs of Melanesian origin ... folksongs, were considered rustic.'[35] West Papuan dance is energetic and heated, contrasting with Indonesian dance which is generally more controlled and minimalist. According to Luther, Indonesians perceived bare-breasted dancers to be shameful, and feisty dancing to be threatening as it invoked resistance. It was not that West Papuan dancing was prohibited by the state, explained Luther, it was just not actively supported. Luther's observation follows other commentators who have suggested that in Indonesia, 'primitive' people and their arts do not disappear because of progress, 'rather, they are *made* to disappear as a result, sometimes unintended, of government policies'.[36]

Photo 2. Arnold Ap (seated fourth from the right) and fellow Mambesak musicians, c. 1981.

Photo: Marthen Rumabar.

Mambesak performed an oral narrative known as *mop* in an era when there was no field of published West Papuan literature. In this period, Ulli Beier published two volumes of indigenous writing from PNG, including the writer John Kasaipwalova whose play 'My brother my enemy' is mentioned in Chapter 9.[37] Yet there was not a single West Papuan inclusion in an anthology of 60 Indonesian writers titled *Blue sea blue sky* edited by Rosidi.[38] The form of *mop* may be a short vignette or dialogue between two characters, and its subject is often a moral commentary on a particular event or social interaction. *Mop* is written and performed in the Irian dialect, claimed to 'truly touch the ear and heart of the people'[39] and 'tap the feelings of rural Irianese'.[40] By Irian dialect, I refer to Suharno's research which distinguished Standard Indonesian from Indonesian spoken in Irian Jaya, in terms of phonology, morphology, syntax and lexicon.[41]

Kapissa distinguished between 'street *mop*' and 'art *mop*'.[42] Street *mop* is categorised as shallow, objectifying people for the sake of entertainment. Whereas art *mop* resembles a religious parable mirroring aspects of social life:

> [through *mop*] a heart which is unscrupulous may be corrected, excessive ambition bridled, power which is corrupt restricted, greedy appetite controlled. This is important, for the creation of a human earth that is imperishable and eternal in this land.[43]

Mop's humourous veil enables its performance and circulation in spite of its political subject matter of scruples, ambition, power and greed. Its meaning is often esoteric: to know *mop* is to know local social life intimately. Mambesak performed *mop* on the program 'Pinang stall' broadcast on Radio Republik Indonesia in Jayapura. *Mop* continue to be published in the daily column 'Papeda stall' of the *Cenderawasih Post*. It is fitting that it has been performed in shows, and published in columns that reference practices stereotyped as distinctly West Papuan i.e., the eating of *papeda* made from sago, and the chewing of betelnut or *pinang*. (Although it ought to be qualified that sago is also consumed in parts of Eastern Indonesia, and betelnut is chewed across the archipelago.)

George Aditjondro passed me several examples of *mop* written by Arnold Ap, published in the newsletter titled *Serikat* in 1983. Below is my translation of the *mop* 'Asnat cries':

> Christmas Day. Asnat is holidaying at her uncle's village. There is no electricity. There are no kiosks. Completely dark just like Efrata [a quarter in Bethlehem mentioned in the Bible]. Everyone enters church. Some wear clothes and some merely wear *sarung katotor*. There are more people without clothes than there are with clothes. The time arrives to light the tree. But there are no candles. In her heart, Asnat thinks: in the city, there are electricity, candles and paper that go to waste. If it was sent here, it could be used. After praying, an elder divided potatoes, meat and drinking water. Everyone ate joyfully except Asnat. Asnat cried. Her uncle thought Asnat was playing, so he sang in jest: '1 2 3 1 5 4 3 4 5. Why are you crying dear Asnat?' Asnat said: 'It's nothing uncle, I feel bad seeing the children without clothes, and not eating cake or drinking tea.' Her uncle laughed: 'Here it is usual. The congregation is happy and praises God. Why should you cry? You should give thanks that you can experience such a simple, calm, wise and peaceful Christmas. Just like the environment in Bethlehem, Efrata.' Asnat reflected: 'If I become an important person [e.g., a government official], every Christmas I will send clothes, sugar and cake to the village so that the children can feel like they have friends in the city.'

'Asnat cries' can be read as a vignette which uses the commonplace binary village:town to elaborate deprivations and neglect of the village through failed development, or lack of development activity, and comparative excesses of the town (cake and sweet tea are like champagne and caviar). Asnat's uncle instructs his niece that people in the village are simple and devout. He relates the village analogously to the holy quarter of Efrata in Bethlehem and does not indulge his city niece's pity. Instead, he invites her to see village life through a different lens. It is possible that Ap means to map cultural West Papuans onto village, and multi-ethnic 'Irian Jayans', including migrants, onto town. In this case, the village might represent a cultural state prior to colonisation. For example, Asnat's concern about the wearing of *sarong katotor* recalls the state's *koteka* campaign in the province of Jayawijaya, which attempted to replace the *koteka* with trousers.[44] Undoubtedly this *mop* romanticises village life, but it also lends integrity (honesty, devotion) to village West Papuans usually characterised as backwards and naive. The story reminds urban West Papuans living in multi-ethnic towns of the geographical territory of their birthplace which distinguishes them from migrants.

Mop and song recordings of Mambesak were embraced by West Papuan listeners. Their songs were sung at parties and festivals, and broadcast by the government's rural development programme. Between 1978 and 1983, Mambesak recorded five volumes of folksongs from nine regions. The lyrics were transcribed in the 1980 songbook *Collection of folk songs of Irian Jaya* and cassettes were marketed throughout the province. Mambesak's output was prolific and it performed 187 live broadcasts on Radio Republik Indonesia's 'Rainbow of Cultures', a program promoting 'unity in diversity'.

After leaving Mambesak in 1980, Ap's collaborator Sam Kapissa went on to develop a music industry on the island of Biak that boasted at least 10 recording groups, and produced thousands of cassettes for distribution.[45] Performance groups also proliferated throughout the northern region of Irian Jaya during this period. Groups comprised students and civil servants, and most made recordings. In a dominated political environment, dancing a dance of familiar local origin to music played by local performers using *tifa* and ukelele among people considered 'us' was affective. Collectivism is embodied in the progression or form of a dance,[46] and in audience formation. Dancing while singing in one's own regional language further intensifies the experience. Yohanes explained this eloquently: 'When we hear songs sung in our regional language it is like it is our own flag that is waving. To hear the lyrics of a song in one's own language outside of one's place is enough to make that person weep.'

In the early 1980s, Mambesak members were targeted for interrogation. In July 1982, after a group of Cenderawasih University students raised the West Papuan flag outside the Provincial Assembly building in Jayapura, Arnold Ap was arrested under suspicion of instigating the event but was later released without being charged.[47] In September 1983, the family of Mambesak member Alex Mebri was interrogated, and his father was executed in public by Indonesian soldiers.[48] Later, Mambesak technical coordinator Constant Ruhukail was arrested and detained in relation to the accusation that a lawyer called Henk di Suvero had been guided to an interview with OPM leaders in the jungle.[49] On 30 November 1983 Ap was arrested on suspicion of several charges: arranging contact between di Suvero and an OPM leader; funding the flight into PNG of Cenderawasih University (UNCEN) lecturer Fred Hatabu and OPM leader Seth

Rumkorem from the profits of Mambesak recordings; and assisting in the preparation of documentation for other West Papuans planning to flee into PNG.[50]

The Military Commander of Irian Jaya claimed that Ap had confessed that Mambesak songs were intended to inspire West Papuan resistance to Indonesian rule.[51] According to Aditjondro, Ap had proposed that Mambesak music be played in villages on the Indonesian–PNG border to encourage OPM guerillas to leave the jungle and return to their own villages to the west.[52] The implication is that Mambesak music invokes nostalgia for place. The Indonesian military also alleged that a network of OPM sympathisers operated from within UNCEN and other government offices, supporting resistance activities of West Papuan soldiers who had deserted the Indonesian military and were hiding out in the jungle.

Ap continued to produce and record from prison. Another Mambesak member visited him there, 'sometimes staying till late at night chatting, singing and making recordings'.[53] Ap was allowed his guitar, tape-recorder and cassettes, and he understood this favourable treatment in terms of the Biak proverb: 'Feed your enemy well before you kill him.'[54] The lyrics of 'I am sailing away' suggest that Ap anticipated his fate:

> I am sailing away
> I am sailing away (to make my way)
> To the place where the sun rises
> To look for knowledge as a foothold in life for the time to come
> Clouds at the peak of the blue mountain
> Sad hearted but joyful
> In the land of my ancestors
> On a certain day tomorrow
> I imagine the suffering of my people/nation
> Mother, Father as well as people
> That earthly land I leave behind with great yearning.

(Translated from the Biak language into Indonesian by Luther.)

Writing in the Biak language, Ap concealed the song's meaning from prison guards. In it, he establishes his nativeness by mentioning his place as ancestral, and recalls his people's colonisation by mentioning their suffering. Using a culturally stylised island metaphor of sea journey, he sails away from this world for a 'heavenly' other.

On 26 April 1984, Arnold Ap was killed by soldiers allegedly as he escaped from jail where he had been detained since his arrest.[55] His death occurred against a backdrop of political uprising that had resulted in heavy reprisals by the Indonesian military: house-to-house searches in urban areas; sweeping activity in rural areas; and counter-insurgency activities on the PNG border deploying thousands of Indonesian ground troops and airforce equipment.[56] Seventeen years later, in an obituary of Sam Kapissa who had been anthropologist Danilyn Rutherford's interlocutor, Rutherford paralleled Kapissa's courage to survive for a cause with Ap's courage to die for it.[57] Following Ap's death, students did not go to the Cenderawasih campus for months. Those who arrived were fingerprinted and photographed.[58] Some students returned to their villages of origin in order to conceal themselves, others fled to Vanimo, PNG. Remaining Mambesak members were told by the authorities that if they wished to perform publicly they must 'sing not of Papuan culture, but of the unity of Indonesia'.[59]

At the time of fleeing Jayapura for Vanimo in February 1984, Luther took great risks to enter Ap's office at the Cenderawasih University Museum and remove the original mastercopies of the Mambesak recordings, and a large dual tape recorder. Luther carried only these things in his flight to Vanimo. In August 1984 at Blackwater camp, Vanimo, West Papuan musicians formed a group called 'Sampari', meaning 'Morning Star' in the Biak language. From their site of exile, they arranged and recorded songs categorised as 'songs of the struggle' such as 'Blue 7 White 6', which refers to the stripes on the West Papuan flag. At East Awin in 1989, Sampari held several performances and were well received by other refugees. Gradually members dispersed, leaving East Awin for other cities in PNG and the Netherlands where some were offered third country asylum. In 1998, a member of a Netherlands-based group called 'Mambesak' visited East Awin. During the band member's visit, northerners talked about the formation of an art and culture youth group at East Awin to be called 'Mambesak'. Luther was critical of the proposal:

> Mambesak cannot be used arbitrarily as a name nor is it something personally owned. The spirit of Mambesak must follow the spirit of Arnold Ap, i.e., open. Everyone must be permitted to join. Mambesak is a symbol of West Papua, not just the island of Biak, and it must not be a family enterprise but rather a national thing otherwise it will insult Arnold Ap's memory and be without basis. Also, it must have performance expertise and ought to consult original Mambesak members.

Luther's rebuke identified Ap and Mambesak as public cultural icons, and original members as custodians of sorts.

Ap was not an entirely secular figure to many Biak West Papuans. Some likened him to a Biak prophet figure known as *konor*:

> In English, *konor* would translate as a philosopher, or a saint, who had many powers. These people always think good thoughts, have a true understanding of life and can even foresee the future. For example, Arnold predicted his own death well in advance. He knew that his

destiny was inevitable. In that regard you could make a comparison with the death of Christ.[60]

Ap could 'spark fire' in others,[61] and could even make Koreri 'live again'.[62] In Biak terms *'konor'* is a person who receives divine inspiration from Manarmakeri, or God in the Biak language. Koreri refers to a religious-political movement of the north coast of Irian Jaya based on the expected return of a mythical figure called Manarmakeri. Koreri is also used as a metaphor for heaven, and a calm harbour where there is neither wind nor wave. Protestant pastor and anthropologist Kamma, whose monograph on Koreri is seminal, proposed that elements of the Bible were incorporated into the Koreri mythical sphere and that efforts were made to prove the congruity between the Koreri ideal and the Bible.[63] Rutherford however, suggests that believers claim the myth of Manarmakeri as the Bible's secret source: like the Old Testament narrative it reveals a man blessed with a son in his old age, and like the New Testament, it depicts a virgin birth.[64]

The Koreri movement remains meaningful for some people from Biak-Numfoor, Serui and Manokwari living at East Awin. They narrated the legend of Koreri in historical terms, recounting the story of Mansar as a history of the Biak people and relating themselves to the territorial traces of Mansar's existence. The notion of 'an ideal state' contained in Koreri, like the Bible, allows West Papuans to imagine a liberated world. Kamma wrote that nationalistic aspirations and opposition to foreigners became part of the list of expectations connected with Koreri.[65] The logic of Ap as *konor* and Mambesak as Koreri movement is like this: if Ap's musical composition, leadership and following was considered to be bequeathed by Mansar or God, then this recognition of him as *konor* would manifest in the emergence of a Koreri movement, conceivably, Mambesak. The posthumous veneration of Ap as *konor* is analogous to the canonising of a person as a Christian saint.

At the time of Ap's death in 1984 many of his peers were living at Vanimo, across the border from Jayapura. They were subsequently relocated to the inland refugee settlement at East Awin. At the time of my fieldwork, the circumstances of Ap's death were readily recounted by those who had known him. Like the historical narratives of the previous chapter, narratives about Ap's death are constructed in terms of a rubric of colonisation. In the following account of Ap's last performance told by most northerners at East Awin, it is Ap's West Papuanness (and perhaps his Biakness) that is violated by the Indonesian state. The state's denial of matters of cultural importance to West Papuans underwrites a fundamental antagonism and basis of their struggle for nationhood:

> In November 1983 at a Mambesak performance in the Parliament
> building, Jayapura, military officials from Jakarta led by the Minister
> of Defence, and guests from other nations including India, Korea and

America, were invited by Mambesak members to dance the Yospan. Then the wife of the Minister for Defence [General Murdani] asked Ap for his bird of paradise headdress. According to custom, feathers ought not be requested nor given but Ap gave her the feather. He made the comment that perhaps the gift would get him out of trouble at a later time. While Mambesak members ate outside, Ap remained inside speaking intensely with the international guests. Later in the taxi journey on the way home, he told his wife that she must be prepared for the worst. He was arrested the following day.

The standardised account of Ap's final performance places him and Mambesak in an international setting where Ap plays the role of statesman, and the provincial Yospan dance is showcased at a national function for international recognition. The request by Murdani's wife shows the state's disdain for local custom and attitude towards cultural artefacts as souvenirs. Ap's surrender of the bird of paradise feather is portrayed as a violation of custom which results in his capture. It is the culture of the gift which is violated, for Ap's gift is met with capture rather than reciprocity. The narrative juxtaposes customary local belief against the state. Narrators explained that Ap was offended by the request because he respected the north coast custom that proscribed the wearing of bird of paradise feathers by anyone who was not a tribal leader or *ondoafi*.

Ap's peers had also known his cross-cousin Eduard Mofu. They recounted the event of Ap's death in terms of his *nafirem* or cross-cousin relation with Mofu. Ap's father was Mofu's maternal uncle, his mother's brother. Mofu's own father had also been killed by Indonesian soldiers. It was explained to me that the relation between cross-cousins is more intimate than that between siblings, and resembles the relation between male in-laws. It is described by Rutherford: 'In the heat of battle, a man will leave his dying brother and flee to safety, but if his cross-cousin has fallen, he will perish by his side … Cross-cousins cannot bring themselves to step over each other's feet, but brothers can fight to the death.'[66] By offering Mofu freedom if he abandoned Ap, the state attempted to negate Mofu's cross-cousin obligation and pitted a customary familial relationship against the state. People did not explain why Mofu was arrested, only that he was offered freedom but chose to stay:

> Ap's cousin Edu Mofu was imprisoned with him. Mofu chose to remain despite the offer of his own release. Mofu's tortured body was dumped at sea. Had Mofu abandoned Ap their relatives would say: 'You forgot your cousin. Between *nafirem* it is like this: if he dies, I must also die.' Mofu had to intervene or his parent would ask of him, where is your brother? One heavy burden to bear.

After Ap's death, Mambesak member Constan Ruhukail wrote and circulated a five-page essay on the circumstances of Ap's death, and the contribution of his work. Ruhukail wrote that the state's reaction to Ap's project revealed the boundaries of the government's own culture project.[67] Ap's work was apparently in line with the Indonesian state's inventorying of provincial cultures towards a unified national culture, but his motivations were divergent. Mambesak's performance repertoire was culturally bounded, limited to songs and dances considered traditional, and originating from within West Papua. The bounded nature of the repertoire imagined a certain cultural congruity, and an overarching cultural West Papuanness—an alternative identity.

ENDNOTES

[1] Anderson, p. 178.

[2] George Aditjondro, *Cahaya Bintang Kejora: Papua Barat dalam kajian sejarah, budaya, ekonomi, dan hak asasi manusia*, Elsham, Jakarta, 2000, pp. 5–37.

[3] Appadurai, p. 15.

[4] Appadurai, p. 15.

[5] Appadurai, p. 162.

[6] Appadurai, p. 13.

[7] Appadurai, p. 46.

[8] Appadurai, p. 46.

[9] Edward Wolfers, 'West Irian 1: The Bird of Paradise State University', *Institute of Current World Affairs Newsletter*, 1969, p.18.

[10] D. C. Ajamiseba and A. J. Subari, 'Pengabdian pada masyarakat di Universitas Cenderawasih, disampaikan dalam seminar Lokakarya', unpublished report, Cenderawasih University, Jayapura, 1983.

[11] Anderson, p. 178.

[12] Aditjondro, *Cahaya Bintang Kejora*, pp. 5–37.

[13] Paul Taylor, 'The *nusantara* concept of culture: local traditions and national identity as expressed in Indonesia's museums', in Paul Taylor (ed.), *Fragile traditions: Indonesian art in jeopardy*, University of Hawai'i Press, Honolulu, 1994, pp. 71–90.

[14] Appadurai, p. 39.

[15] Hughes-Freeland, 'Indonesian image enhancement, *Anthropology Today*, 5, 6, 1989, pp. 3–5.

[16] Hughes-Freeland, p. 3.

[17] Hughes-Freeland, p. 5.

[18] Arnold Ap, 'Inventarisasi gerak dasar tari daerah Irian Jaya', in Don Flassy (ed.), *Aspek dan prospek Seni Budaya Irian Jaya*, Cenderawasih University, Jayapura, 1974, p. 117.

[19] Greg Acciaioli, 'Culture as art: from practice to spectacle in Indonesia', *Canberra Anthropology*, 8, 1&2, pp. 148-172.

[20] Kathryn Robinson, 'The platform house: expression of a regional identity in the modern Indonesian nation', in V. M. Hooker (ed.), *Culture and society in New Order Indonesia*, Oxford University Press, Oxford, 1993, p. 229.

[21] Rutherford, 'Remembering Sam Kapissa,' pp. 16–17.

[22] Arnold Ap, 'Death and mourning among the Keenok', in M. Walker (ed.) *Asmat Papers I*, Cenderawasih University, Jayapura, 1974, pp. 57–73; Ap, 'Magic and Sorcery among the Keenok', in M. Walker (ed.) *Asmat Papers I*, Cenderawasih University, Jayapura, 1974, pp. 74–90; Ap, 'Beberapa aspek kebudayaan material Keenok', in M. Walker (ed.) *Asmat Papers I*, Cenderawasih University, Jayapura, 1974, pp. 221–33; Ap, 'Seni ukir Teluk Geelvink (Teluk Saerera)', in D. A. L Flassy (ed.) *Aspek dan prospek seni budaya Irian Jaya*, Pemda tingkat I Jayapura, Jayapura, 1983, pp.169–82; Arnold Ap and Sam Kapissa, 'Seni patung daerah Irian Jaya', *Lembaga Antropologi*, Jayapura, 1981; Arnold Ap and J. R. Mansoben, 'Membuat perahu Asmat', in M. Walker (ed.) *Asmat Papers II*, Cenderawasih University, Jayapura, 1974, pp. 62–75; Arnold Ap and W. G. Solheim, 'Pottery manufacturing in Abar, Lake Sentani Irian Jaya', *Irian*, 6, 1, 1977, pp. 52–70.

[23] Ap, 'Inventarisasi gerak'.

[24] Ap, 'Inventarisasi gerak', p. 122.

[25] Ap, 'Inventarisasi gerak', p. 123.

[26] Ap, 'Inventarisasi gerak', p. 123.

[27] George Aditjondro, pers. comm., November 1999; cf. Danilyn Rutherford, 'Of birds and gifts: revising tradition on an Indonesian frontier', *Cultural Anthropology*, 11, 4, 1996, p. 590.

[28] Sam Kapissa, 'Randan' yang di Indonesiakan', *Oikoumene*, 1983, pp. 31–2.

[29] Aditjondro, 'Karya dan Gema 'Mambesak' di Irian Jaya', *Oikoumene*, 1984, pp. 27–30.

[30] Aditjondro, pers. comm., November 1999.

[31] Aditjondro, 'Karya dan Gema', pp. 29–30.

[32] Sawaki, pers. comm., 2001.

[33] Merauke Committee, 'Data sejarah Papua Barat dari tahun 1511 s/d tahun 1998', unpublished manuscript, 1998, p. 29.

[34] Danilyn Rutherford, 'Raiding the land of the foreigners: power, history and difference in Biak, Irian Jaya', PhD thesis, Cornell University, 1997, p. 263.

[35] Tom Ireeuw, 'Arnold Ap autobiography', *West Papua Bulletin*, 3, 1994.

[36] Original italics. Shelley Errington, 'Unraveling narratives', in Paul Taylor (ed.), *Fragile traditions: Indonesian art in jeopardy*, University of Hawai'i Press, Honolulu, 1994, p. 142.

[37] Ulli Beier, *Black writing from New Guinea*, University of Queensland Press, Brisbane, 1973; *Voices of Independence*, University of Queensland Press, Brisbane, 1980.

[38] David Hill, 'Suara Kemerdekaan: tulisan hitam baru dari Papua Niugini', *Kompas*, 2 November 1980, p. 8.

[39] Irja-DISC, Nomination letter to the Indonesian Department of Population and Environment for annual prize for outstanding contribution to environmental conservation (Kalpataru).

[40] Ajamiseba and Subari, p. 13.

[41] I. Suharno, 'Some notes on the teaching of standard Indonesian to speakers of Irianese Indonesian', *Irian*, 8, 1, 1979, pp. 3–32.

[42] Sam Kapissa, 'Budaya "Mop" sebagai media pesan', *Serikat*, November–December 1983, p. 5.

[43] Kapissa, 'Budaya "Mop"', p. 5.

[44] C. Budiardjo and L. Soei Liong, *West Papua: the obliteration of a people* (third edition), TAPOL, Surrey, England, 1988, pp. 56–7; Nonie Sharp, *The rule of the sword*, Kibble Books, Malmsbury, Victoria, 1977, p. 25.

[45] Aditjondro, *Cahaya Bintang Kejora*, pp. 122–5.

[46] Gillian Bottomley, *From another place: migration and the politics of culture*, Cambridge University Press, Cambridge, 1992, pp. 72–3.

[47] Smith, pp. 173–4.

[48] Smith, p. 174.

[49] Smith, pp. 174–5.

[50] Aditjondro, *Cahaya Bintang Kejora*, pp. 5–37.

[51] Budiardjo and Liong, pp. 126–7.

[52] Aditjondro, *Cahaya Bintang Kejora*, pp. 5–37.

[53] Budiardjo and Liong, p. 28.

[54] Ireeuw.

[55] Budiardjo and Liong, pp. 125–36; Constan Ruhukail, 'Kasus pembunuhan Arnold C. Ap dan Eddy Mofu', *Berita Tanpa Sensor*, Gerakan demi hak-hak asasi manusia dan demokrasi, Leiden, 1985; Aditjondro, *Cahaya Bintang Kejora*, pp. 138–56.

[56] Robin Osborne, *Indonesia's secret war: the guerilla struggle in Irian Jaya*, Allen & Unwin, Sydney, p. 100.

[57] Rutherford, 'Remembering Sam Kapissa,' pp. 16–17.

[58] George Aditjondro, 'Perkembangan keadaan tahanan eks-panorama', unpublished, n. d.

[59] Osborne, p. 153.

[60] Rumakiek quoted in Osborne, p. 149.

[61] Ireeuw.

[62] Kaisiepo in Sharp, *The Morning Star in Papua Barat*, p. 64.

[63] F. C. Kamma, *Koreri: Messianic movements in the Biak-Numfoor culture area*, Martinus Nijhoff, The Hague, p. 282.

[64] Rutherford, 'Raiding the land', p. 415.

[65] Kamma, p. 280.

[66] Rutherford, 'Raiding the land', p. 173.

[67] Ruhukail.

Chapter 3

A flight path

Mambesak members once danced semi-clothed as a statement against the Indonesian government's Koteka Operation which aimed to eliminate aspects of highland culture, including the wearing of the *koteka* or penis gourd. The *koteka* has ambiguous meanings. Some Indonesians refer to West Papuan people as '*koteka*'. In this context it is a pejorative exonym, reifying West Papuan people as a category. (Although *koteka* is only worn by highlander men.) Yet *koteka* is also an object that marks out non-Indonesianness, for there are no other *koteka* wearers in the Indonesian archipelago. *Koteka* signifies Melanesianness, as it is worn in several places across the entire highland band of the island of New Guinea.

Critics of the 1970s Koteka Operation interpreted it as an attempt by the state to emasculate highlander resistance, because the cultural traditions of highlander warriors were threatening.[1] Supporters of the Koteka Operation described it in benign terms. For example, the Institute of Anthropology's *Irian: Bulletin of West Irian* published an article titled 'The Koteka Operation: an effort to hasten development in the interior region of West Irian.'[2] The author, an Indonesian anthropologist employed by the Institute and seconded to the staff of the operation, framed it in terms of development:

> ... the government together with the armed forces in West Irian have initiated a development project called Operasi Koteka ... aimed at helping the people [in the Central Highlands] to upgrade their economy and social conditions by providing practical training in such matters as improved gardening methods, animal breeding, better housing, health, hygiene and so on.[3]

The particular formulation of the Koteka Operation can be linked to the crisis of the modern nation-state. Because a polity is considered legitimate if it is founded on a natural affinity in spite of its multi-ethnic setting, the Indonesian nation-state undertakes projects such as the Koteka Operation in an effort to produce group affinity. By tying Baliem peoples' bodily practices like hygeine, cleanliness and health to other Indonesians, the campaign sought to make group affinity an embodied experience.[4]

Living next door to me at East Awin was a Dani woman who had fled the Baliem Valley in 1977 during the Koteka Operation and other military campaigns. Katarina ran a kiosk from her house, selling small quantities of items like kerosene, razor blades, fishing line, gas lantern wicks, rice and salt. On several occasions I heard her recount anecdotes of her flight in 1977. I asked if she would be willing to recount the entire narrative for my research. I notated her narrative, which was spoken in Indonesian, in a single afternoon's session. The form is linear and chronological, in fact it literally begins by marking time and place. Katarina's starting point is a sequence of events that occurred in her locality prior to flight in 1977. Her end point is 1984 when she made it safely across the international border into PNG. It is possible that her linear narrative had been coached, for this was not the first telling. The final lines make this explicit: 'I want my story written down. Jeronimus [religious leader] has already recorded it. All the stories of suffering have been collected and sent to Geneva.'

On that afternoon, Katarina pulled the shutter down low over the kiosk window at the front of the house, and we retreated to the cooler rear of the house where we sat on empty rice sacks, our backs to the wall. Katarina spoke slowly in Indonesian using simple short sentences—perfect for my method of hand-written notation. It precluded me from recording my own spontaneous, clarifying questions however. To avoid interrupting her narrative, I chose not to record either my own questions or Katarina's responses. At the time of notation, I had not considered side comments or non-verbal gestures to be integral to the main narrative. It was only retrospectively that I realised such comments offered critical emotional dynamics to the text. For example, several times in the course of the narrative Katarina dramatically stopped speaking. Shaking her head and biting her clenched hand, she exclaimed: 'I am scared all over again.' This was lost in my transcription but it would not have been if I had produced a full transcript including my clarifying questions, and Katarina's responses. A full transcript makes more explicit the interviewer's hand, and the process of the transcription. At East Awin, I tape-recorded song, but never speech. Very early in the research I judged the historical moment of my research to be tenuous. The people I interviewed were in the throes of decision-making about return to the homeland. I figured that the last thing they wanted in the event of their return was testimonial evidence of their political lives in someone else's hands.

Katarina's slow, measured speech allowed me to transcribe the narrative almost verbatim. But it was difficult to elicit phrasing from her intonation and rhythm, and I punctuated the piece independently after translation. The imperative of constant movement in the narrative is driven in repetitions like 'walking, walking, walking' and 'chasing, chasing, chasing'. To retain a sense of movement, and avoid compartmentalising the narrative, I have not constructed paragraphs. I have tried to capture the uninterrupted, sometimes breathless, character of the monologue. It contains a fundamental tension between stillness and movement. Movement can reveal your position, for if you move you could die and in stillness there is concealment. Yet movement can also distance you from the enemy, and stillness can bring the enemy closer to you.

After news spread that I had recorded Katarina's story, two Dani men at East Awin requested that I record their narratives to provide them with a written record of their account in English. These men recounted their flight from the Baliem Valley to PNG as a meticulously dated chronology of battles, departures and arrivals. Dramatic events punctuated their journey, but the narrators did not elaborate the time or space between these events. There was brief commentary about incidents that were disturbing like the dilemma of unburied corpses, accidental drownings that occurred while fording flooded river crossings, and the capture and murder of Dani spies working for Indonesia. In contrast, Katarina's narrative is fine-grained and sensuous. It invokes Dani cosmology at every turn and offers insights into the meaning of displacement and emplacement, and the religious character of nationalist thinking.

Katarina's narrative reveals Dani belief in animals like the bat, mountain dog and dragon snake as Lord of the earth spirits, alongside belief in a Christian God. According to the narrative, both landlord spirits and God enabled Dani survival during the period of flight. The discovery of food such as human-sized fish during famine is represented in miraculous terms. Belief in God is protective and those who 'forgot' God died in the jungle. Didactism is at play too: 'We prayed over and over. We must not forget prayer.' The narrative resonates with the proposition in West Papuan nationalist discourse that God supports liberation. Katarina distinguishes between God and pastors as mere agents. Her suspicion of the pastor's motives underscores a generalised West Papuan sentiment of Dutch betrayal. The pastor's own congregation mocks him when he attempts to play the millenial card by predicting a date for the miracle of independence. The pastor is an ambiguous character. On the one hand he casts Katarina and her fellow fugitives as followers of Satan because of their armed resistance to the Indonesian nation-state. The implication is that he supports the project of the nation-state to incorporate Dani as Indonesian citizens. Yet he seems to encourage their resistance by his gesture of rolling a handful of soil into a marble, invoking an archetype of primordialism—a 'trope of the tribe'.[5] Katarina's husband also defines himself using other primordia of kinship and race: 'I am an original person. I am the one who is a landholder. I have black skin.' Katarina's husband identifies colonisation as anachronistic: 'Every [colonised] country is already independent why can't I be?'

Outside the Baliem Valley of their homeland, Dani displacement is signified by a landscape which is grotesque in its foreignness: paths are layered with leeches, fish are dense in the water, cassava is fleshless, insects invade the body. Displacement is also signified by their starvation in a different ecosystem: 'People died little by little. In the morning someone died. In the afternoon someone died. In the night someone died … What could we eat?' Lack of cultural knowledge means they cannot process foods like sago and coconut, and do not recognise forest food that is gathered. Displacement is also signified by the skin disease *kaskado* (grille), present in the people of Mamberamo and PNG. Katarina has previously known it as a mange disease in dogs. In people it is as foreign as sago, and sago smells rotten like *kaskado*. Starvation and fatigue are preferable than return to the homeland though. The Indonesian military occupation of the Baliem Valley has altered the homeland. Return to their own valley is a more frightening prospect than flight into foreign territory: 'We could see our valley from afar. But we were afraid to enter—afraid to enter the Indonesian region.'

Indonesian warfare tactics target everything that is culturally meaningful to Dani everyday life: their *honai* or homes are burned, their pigs slaughtered, their gardens and fruiting trees trashed. Describing Dani prospects against the power of the Indonesian military, Katarina uses the analogy of a fishing bomb that brings concealed fish immediately to the surface of the water, stone dead or stunned: 'We were like a school of fish swimming around and the soldiers used poison. Like the masses of dead fish that surface when a fishing bomb is used …' The Indonesians use helicopters, aeroplanes and bombs against Dani spears, cassowary bone knives and a Makassarese bayonet. Initially, Dani people did not even recognise the sound of Indonesian planes. In another setting, Katarina had told me:

> People ventured outside to cut bananas. They re-entered their *honai*. Some had eaten, others were still eating. Our parents did not recognise the war planes. They thought it was assistance promised by the OPM. They were like pigs who did not know the noise of dogs. They stood in the clearings. The plane dived like an eagle. Some died in their houses. Others died in the places where they stood. Others were wounded. Others hid in their houses and burned to death. It was an air attack by three fighter planes.

Acts of slaughter in Katarina's narrative are gratuituous and without morality. Neither innocent children nor defenceless people in the course of prayer are immune.

It is not entirely a narrative of defeat, for Katarina also speaks of adaptation, tactic and survival. Pursued by soldiers, Dani call on their own ancestral spirits—mountain dogs and forest bats—to indicate the path and caution danger. Starving, they learn how to process the pith of the sago tree to replace their sweet potato as staple. They also learn how to get at the creamy flesh inside a coconut shell. They reinvent themselves from sedentary gardeners to forest gatherers. They learn how to manoeuvre canoes among coastal crocodiles, how to placate malevolent ancestral spirits and how to read signs of their own trespassing. They radically adjust their burial custom to the new environment, wrapping corpses in palm leaves rather than burying them below the ground. They establish meaningful and productive relationships with villagers by exchanging their own meagre belongings for food. With the sun's position as compass plotting their easterly journey, they navigate their way across an international boundary into the neighbouring state to seek 'refuge' at last. But a sense of disorientation is sustained in Katarina's account. Her mother has severed her finger in a customary sign of grief for her missing daughter presumed dead, and 'buries' her by holding the ceremony that commemorates the deceased 40 days after burial. Katarina can remember her parents' names, but not those of her siblings:

On May 2, 1977, at Karubaga, the OPM closed ABRI's airfield by laying tree trunks end to end. Aeroplanes could not enter. They wanted to be the only ones there. Drums were beaten. There was a pilot who usually supplied rice to civil servants. He began his descent through a thick cloud. The pilot was asked: 'Do you work for Indonesia or alone?' Raising his hands, the pilot replied: 'O, I work for myself, I am bringing rice.' People took the rice. The pilot was taken to the Dutch Pastor who released him. The airfield was still shut. A helicopter landed on the site of the hospital to airlift the pilot. Houses and kiosks were ransacked. The army could not land. Helicopters airlifted foreigners including people from other places in Irian. I ran to my parents' village. An ABRI helicopter from Wamena arrived. We thought a bomb would be dropped. We entered the jungle wearing black. A last meal of potatoes was eaten. All of the children were gathered together. The helicopter dropped a letter. It read: 'OPM is prohibited. All must come in and surrender.' The Pastor sent a letter to us. It read: 'Local people of this place, listen to your father: white-skinned people have cleared the field. Listen to your father. In twelve nights we will meet.' People were scared the pastor was colluding with ABRI. They slept outside. Five times the letter came and people did not go because they feared deception. Then the Pastor came to the village church one Sunday. During the announcements, a member of the congregation proposed that the Pastor had been deceived. The Pastor replied: 'Don't join the OPM, it is satanic. You are not permitted to join. You cannot be independent. Irian is already independent.' The congregation sat and listened patiently for three hours. My husband John spoke up: 'Why do you say I am Satan? I am an original person. I am the one who is a landholder. I have black skin. I am an original child. Every country is already independent why can't I be?' The Pastor then told us that independence would come in 1982. People laughed: 'See, see the white-skinned person tricking.' People felt he was deceiving us because he was playing with words. After praying, the Pastor rubbed a handful of earth into a marble shape and upon placing it in the palm of John's hand, said: 'If you want freedom, if you are indigenous to this place, hold onto this earth.' We took this dirt ball and carried it on the journey to Mamberamo but the rain caused it to disintegrate. The soldiers were looking for us. There was a saying: 'If you move, you die.' People's dreams, visions and signs governed the direction of our movement. John had a nightmare: we went to John's uncle's village pursued by [Indonesian] soldiers. His uncle told the soldiers they had gone elsewhere. The soldiers then asked a child standing nearby who pointed to the roof. We were forced to descend where we were beaten, including the women, for deceiving the soldiers. Rape. It is not like in PNG. Indonesia rapes. Five soldiers were chasing me. Chasing, chasing, chasing. I ran wearing only my underwear. I ran naked through the day. The houses were burned. I slept alongside pigs in a stable for one month living off the food they threw to the pigs in the stable. Open places would reveal me. We had secret gardens and secret houses. We cooked at night to conceal smoke. We concealed our footprints. The army burned *honai* and they dug out gardens; banana plants and pandanus fruit. 'Operation Trash' truly truly destroyed. Everything was chopped down, everything was dug out. After three weeks in the forest we came down to the valley below. My skin was yellow from lack of food. My parents had been told: 'You have a daughter living in the forest; her body is small now.' They had already prepared to send a pig to me in the forest. Shooting, shooting, shooting. Banyan vines were used to scale trees and cross ravines. Houses were burned. A river was crossed. Walking, walking, walking. We came across a garden and took cucumbers. Concealed in the forest. Concealed by relatives beneath other things in their houses. A child revealed my hiding place to the soldiers. They returned to the house. They considered: 'Women don't know politics. Leave her. She means nothing. Detain the men.' I slept in the forest. I was sixteen years old. I had been married just one day. Six stables of pigs were destroyed and the pigs shot. The soldiers ate the pigs. No one slept. They went into the forest. The mayor was from Biak and was an Indonesian spy. The mayor said: 'You cannot stay here.' Like a football field with spectators all around, I sat in the middle with my parents and husband's parents. Like watching soccer. We were told that we could not live here any more. Expelled. The other villagers agreed to expel us. They clapped their hands and chased us out. We slept on the roadside. There was a large battle at Bokondini. One helicopter and four fighter planes. They offloaded bombs but they did not make their targets. Those bombs that did not reach their target were in the hands of God. Non-Christian villages were not protected by God and were bombed. Indonesia, they bombed and bombed. The bombs made large craters in the ground and split trees into two. Many people died. This was Indonesia's work. We could not fetch food; the gardens were in open fields. We could not wear red or white, only black. We used leaves and stood like trees and fetched food quickly. People were killed. We were like a school of fish swimming around and the soldiers used poison. Like the masses of dead fish that surface when fishing bomb is used, we also had many victims. A child's head was cut off and thrown into a fire. Witnesses were killed. People's limbs were cut off. All of the houses and even churches were burned. People praying in church were shot. Small children were caught like chickens and swung by the ankles into a fire. People were killed left and right. All the children were killed. A beautiful girl asked a Dani spy to spare her life and he killed her directly. Babies were placed on top of their dead mothers. Drinking milk, drinking blood; later they died in that place. We hid ourselves, were pursued and hid again. We circled continuously in the forest. A child of seven months died in my stomach. My body was already wrecked. There was no medicine. We slept on the paths. There were many women. The women decided to surrender. Two men accompanied our return. We could see our valley from afar. But we were afraid to enter; afraid to enter the Indonesian region. We feared surrender so we returned to the men in the forest. My husband asked me: 'Why have you returned?' I replied: 'We were scared to surrender. It is our region but we were scared. My fate is the same if we surrender or I flee. You have already paid [bride-price]. I will follow you. If I return and marry someone else I will feel remorse. Where the men die, let their wives die with them.' There is a bird, a small bat that is the friend of Wamena people. Its shrieks in the night brought news of ABRI spies advancing. A woman shrieked also, she had been arrowed. They were closing in. An ice mountain was climbed. We could not move for the cold. Our bodies were cramped; we could not open our hands. Death. They began shooting, shooting, shooting. A Dani spy was captured [by us]. His arms and legs and nose were chopped off and his heart removed. A bible was placed on top of his body. Walking, walking, walking, walking, walking. We were given a Makassarese bayonet and carried cassowary bones as knives. We passed a dog that is a Lord of the Earth , a sort of human being diseased by *kaskado*. Helicopters circled above villages. We crossed a river at Kobakma. We had eaten nothing, only a single cassava and grass. People died little by little. In the morning someone died. In the afternoon someone died. In the night someone died. We did not know how to eat sago. Its leaves and tree, we did not know. We began to bake sago and share it around. What was this stuff? We could not eat it dry. Three weeks passed and we did not know how to eat it. It smelled like *kaskado*. Mamberamo people also had *kaskado* in the shape of eights and nines on their skin. We had not seen mosquitoes before. Many people died. Mamberamo has swamps, you must use a canoe, there is no path to walk. It is a sort of sea. There were many crocodiles. You must not fall asleep in a canoe; many crocodiles. Crocodile meat is a sort of pig meat; tasty and with fat. A crocodile can swallow a person. When the rivers recede, the fish are in layers. Lift them, lift them into the canoe. Many fish. The Mamberamo region is not suitable for mountain people unless you know how to eat sago. But our bodies became emaciated. We did not know how to eat sago. What could we eat? Our parents died and they rotted on the ground: who had the strength to bury them? Mamberamo people gave us canoes. 'What are these?' we asked. They taught us to use a canoe with a paddle. We came from the west of the Baliem Valley. We did not know how to swim and feared drowning. We stood on the bank and cried. Then we prayed and sang hymns and God opened the path. We were in the hands of God. Those who forgot God died there in the jungle. Those who believed and prayed got through. They prepared seven canoes and accompanied us to the mouth of the river. In a sago *dusun*, a Mamberamo woman and man felled the tree and hacked at the sago pith, flushing it with water. We thought that was the food. Everyone laughed. I gathered some in my hands. An old woman said to me: 'Eh! Child, you must not take it like that, it is not right.' That day I first saw sago mattocked. 'Mama, what are you making?' I asked. The water ran down. They sang and I sat and watched. Mama taught me how to harvest sago: harvest like this, flush it like this, mattock like this. These Mamberamo people did not know Malay. We asked them many questions but they did not know Malay. We gestured with our hands instead. At Mamberamo we wrapped corpses in banana palm leaves. We did not cremate or bury corpses. Many people died. We opened a village on the edge of a large river and made shelters. We ate large leaves and breadfruit nuts. There was no food. What could we eat? Mamberamo people did not make gardens, they lived from the forest. We ate raw *genimo* leaves and palm leaf tips. Where could we find meat? Nothing. There were no dogs either. We could not yet harvest sago. One month passed. We ate dried breadfruit nuts and boiled forest leaves. When hungry, families went out onto the path and foraged for breadfruit nuts and picked leaves, walking until they were tired and their feet hurt. We fanned ourselves continuously with bundles of leaves. It was a hot region. Leeches and mosquitoes entered people's noses, genitals, ears and small wounds. Mosquitoes swarmed like a sort of mist. Mosquitos entered pawpaw and bananas. We just let them be. We slept on the sand. We saw cassava—it had no flesh. We picked cassava leaves and boiled them. We were very happy and rushed over to pick them. We vomited continuously, the leaves were toxic. We prayed over and over. We must not forget prayer. The rocks were slippery. We kept walking, walking, walking. There were no people at Mamberamo; no government. We were happy to see canoes. Our clothes were tattered. They gave us cooked sago. Our stomachs were small, our throats dry. We could only drink. We could not eat breadfruit nuts or cooked sago. 'You must buy food, you have beads', they explained. We gave them beads and some items of clothing and they gave us cassava and sago. We exchanged whatever we had on our bodies. Forest [swamp] people cannot give without something in return. Mamberamo people are good people. [However] if you steal from their gardens, they use magic and make your feet swell immediately. They place signs in their gardens and if you go beyond that point you will fall sick. One year passed. In 1978, the landowners agreed to us living there. We explained to the village leader that there was nothing for us to eat. 'You eat sago', he told us. We asked him what he was asking us to eat and he explained that in his language, sago was '*si*'. We learned to process sago and learned to cook *papeda* by heating stones and placing them in a container made from palm bark to boil the water. We used goggles and caught fish. Our appetites had diminished and we would vomit on eating sago. After one year our bodies became healthy once more. We hunted pigs and the local people gave us land to make gardens. We collected soil and made heaps and grew bananas, potatoes and cassava. In December 1978, the question was asked: 'Raise your hand if you wish to journey to the east.' Five families chose to stay in Mamberamo. The rest raised their hands to go to East Irian. We did not know it as PNG; we did not know its people. Only upon reaching the border did we know. We travelled to the east. We grated cassava for the journey. We found our direction by climbing tall trees to find the position of the sun. The forest was dense, there was no path. We did not know the way. We only knew east and west from the rising and setting of the sun. Leeches were in layers on the path. Our breath was short. One person was pulled along by another. People thought they would die tomorrow. I said: 'If I die, place me on top of a tree.' My legs were cramped. I said: 'Safe travels, I am staying here.' They called me, I could not speak to answer. I would remain behind and die. Someone carried me. It was already dark. I thought I had already died and my corpse was being carried. We did not know coconut palms. What was it on top? We picked one. We did not know its taste. We said to the garden's owner: 'We would like very much to eat this tree's fruit.' We gave him a few items of clothing and the owner opened it with a machete; just like that. He then scooped out the contents. We gathered in a circle and tasted it. We used plant roots to kill fish and ate with a reddish-green leafed vegetable called *gede*. God helped us. We were joyous. We stayed like that, just fetching and eating fish for a whole week. We climbed mountains, meeting giant snakes in our path. Upon passing these snakes we uttered farewell. You must not kill [an animal spirit] Lord of the Earth, you must greet it; it is human and can cause ill effects. We descended and climbed hills over and over. We entered a village. They could not give us food—bananas, meat or sago. We asked: 'Is there anything to eat?' We stayed and watched the villagers continue eating. They did not give food to us until it was dark. We gave large beads and each person offered a piece of clothing. We said: 'We are hungry and we ask for sago and meat. We can buy with our own goods.' We gave them a little cash, clothes and beads. In the sago swamps our feet were spiked by thorns. We met a giant snake, an ancestor so large it was coiled five times. We used plant root poison and killed the fish called 'eight fish' as big as a person. We carried fish in our string bags and on our heads for two weeks. Other fish we left behind to rot. We made a raft to cross a river. Cassowaries were abundant. Our joy returned; before we could have perished on the path unnoticed, now villages were spaced closer together. There was a giant snake on the path ahead eating the eggs of the forest hen. Two people walking in front killed the snake and became paralysed themselves and died. To kill a giant snake is prohibited. In a large village we were given rolled tobacco [cigarette] as long as your arm. We did not know how to smoke them. We thought: 'If we do not accept them, they may not give us food later.' Then they gave us a lot of food. We stayed for one month. They gave us food and we gave beads and articles of clothing. We thought: These people have religion. At a cemetery, we gathered saucepans and plates that had been left on graves. We used these to cook food. We were close to a military post; we could hear the noise of gunfire. We knew we were drawing close to the border. We met a hunter on the road. He said that we were heading to 'PNG'. We did not know PNG. At the end of 1979, we reached the border. We opened a barracks and made a garden. There were no local people living nearby; no houses. We raised pigs. We kidnapped a Filipino; he was concealed in my house. I was later arrested for this. Our leader—who was already married—took another woman whose husband then revealed our position to ABRI. We fled into PNG. In 1983 we went down to Vanimo from Bewani. Papua New Guinea [police] had dug up our gardens and chopped down our plants. We feared imprisonment. Eight people were sent back to Jayapura. All the plants were cut. We were chased left and right and climbed trees. We ate only leaves; the gardens had been destroyed. There were no refugees yet. We were chased, we would enter gardens to fetch food and be chased again. Local people beckoned us: come, come. We ran and they chased us. We fled into the forest but were arrested and taken to Vanimo. A nun said to us: 'You have different hair, different skin. People here have *kaskado* on their bodies. Where

are you from?' She gave us medicine and food and spoke pidgin to us.
She said: '*Yupela bilong we*?' We replied: 'We are from the West; the part
where the sun sets.' In 1984, other refugees arrived. We lived at
Blackwater. [Northerner] people arrived by canoe or foot from Jayapura:
only one night's journey. Those of us from Wamena walked on foot for
two years. At Blackwater we ate like civil servants, selling taro and
greens in the Vanimo market and wearing good clothes. My husband
was imprisoned at Rabaul for one and a half years. I protested: 'Who am
I to live with? I am scared to live in town. Have you arrested my husband
so that he dies in prison?' He was released after that. My mother held a
forty-day ceremony in her village [in Wamena] and chopped off her
finger. [But] I was okay; I was in PNG. Our bodies became healthy again.
But we were no longer permitted to live at Blackwater. We were scared
living so close to the border; scared that Indonesia would arrive again.
I only remember my parents' names, not the names of my siblings. I
don't know how many were born after me. We do not know Indonesian
currency; we have already forgotten. Wamena women make string bags
and sell them to raise money. I want my story written down. Jeronimus
[religious leader] has already recorded it. All the stories of suffering have
been collected and sent to Geneva.

ENDNOTES

1 Budiardjo and Liong, pp. 56–7; Nonie Sharp, p. 25.

2 Oskar Siregar, 'Operasi koteka: suatu usaha mempertjepat pembangunan masjarakat pedalaman Irian
Barat' *Irian*, 1, 2, 1972, pp. 54–60 (also at http://www.papuaweb.rog/dlib/irian/1-2.PDF (15 June 2008)).

3 Oskar Siregar, p. 54.

4 Appadurai, p. 157.

5 Appadurai, p. 161.

Chapter 4

Sensing displacement

Katarina did not say *how* she knew that she had crossed the international border into PNG. She said: 'We knew we were drawing close to the border. We met a hunter on the road. He said that we were heading to "PNG". We did not know PNG. At the end of 1979, we reached the border.' Her journey from the highlands of Irian Jaya to the international border took two years to complete. In contrast, most of the refugees at East Awin were Muyu whose *dusun* was located within several days' walking distance from the camp. The location of 'East Awin' refers to the PNG census division of the landowning group, the Awin people. The fact that East Awin lay more or less contigious to Muyu traditional land provoked my curiosity: how did Muyu conceive of their settlement in a UNHCR site given the proximity of their traditional land?

Muyu displacement at East Awin was defined by their existence outside their customary land on their Awin neighbours' land. It was also defined by their location on the far side of a watershed that marked the eastern boundary of Muyu territory. I was introduced to the significance of this particular watershed by an elderly Muyu man at East Awin called Yusuf. A church elder with two wives and an enormous bevy of adult children and grandchildren, Yusuf's approach to living at East Awin was entirely pragmatic. He had planted sago and coconut palms on his arrival, and at the time of my fieldwork his expansive roof was neatly thatched and his family enjoyed sago.

Yusuf used the Yonggom language term '*aknim*' to describe the north-south watershed which separates two principal rivers: the Digul River and its tributaries Kao and Muyu, and the Fly River and its tributary Ok Tedi. He mapped *aknim* by sketching the watershed. Blocking the watershed with coloured Texta, Yusuf drew *aknim* as interstitial, delineating east and west. He told me that in some parts, particularly towards the south, *aknim* is barely distinguishable and is marked by signs. Around the periphery of the watershed trees to the west lean to the east, and vice versa. Muyu people routinely travelled from west to east across the *aknim* in order to hunt in the sparsely populated and abundant region of the Fly River. Traditional communication and trade routes ran west–east, and it was these connections that were more important than those which ran north–south.[1] At the crest or site of the *aknim*, travellers would pause to light a fire of leaves that emitted a noise when burned. Made from leaves like cork, and other branches, the fire was said to guard against the risk of sickness when crossing to the other side of the watershed. According to Yusuf, elephantiasis (lymphatic filariasis) was common in the Digul area to the west, and quite rare in the area of the Fly River. To the west there was little malaria and to the east it was prevalent, and it was said that people to the west were youthful compared to their eastern counterparts who aged prematurely.

Yusuf also mapped hot and cold states onto west and east. Muyu people living in the western part of their region around the Digul River considered that area to be hot, whereas the area to the east around the Fly River was thought to be cold because of its sparse habitation. Yusuf admitted that his interpretation was subjective: 'This question of hot and cold is a matter of conviction or belief only, a feeling.' Using binaries, Yusuf established an agronomic opposition between the west and east of the *aknim*:

> To the west, bananas and taro are large, to the east, small;
> To the west, game is small bodied containing a high quantity of fat and oil, to the east game is large bodied and the fat contains water;
> To the west, seven coconuts yield one litre of cream, to the east twelve coconuts yield this amount, and
> To the west, soil is disease free. In certain places, soil may be baked until hard then eaten. To the east, soil cannot be eaten as it contains too much sand.

Yusuf also used the east and west banks of the Fly and Ok Tedi rivers as spatial markers of different ecological regions. While the bulge of the Fly River constitutes the thalweg or international boundary, Yusuf constructed east and west in terms of species distribution and landscape. He told me there were no eels to the west of the Fly and Ok Tedi, and substantiated this with a story. In the northern Muyu region where the *aknim* emerges near the Arem mountains to the west, a Muyu man who was pursued by an attacker fled to the east. He entered the Alice River where his hiding place in a clump of pandanus was revealed to his pursuers by the *mep mep* call of the white hornbill bird. Upon capture, he assumed the form of an eel. According to Yusuf, eels are only found to the east of the Tedi, Alice and Fly rivers in the Awin region. I was told that if an eel appears in the Muyu region it is considered a sign of bad luck. By way of illustration, an eel may be demanded as part of a compensation payment claimed by relatives or in-laws of a deceased person. The request is made to deliberately burden the family of the accused as the eel is not found locally and its value is higher than a live pig. Yusuf's second example of ecological distribution pertains to birds. To the west of the Fly, the bird of paradise is golden-yellow, short-bodied and makes the sound *kong kong kon*. To the east it is dark red and sings *ke kokokoko*. Yusuf's third example mentions caves and springs. To the west there are spring-fed streams and vast caves that stretch westward, and to the east there are no springs and streams flow after rain. (Caves to the west were mentioned as places where corpses—victims of the Indonesian military and the OPM—were concealed.)

Unlike the bird of paradise, the afternoon bird is found across the Muyu and Awin regions. In a song titled 'The edge of the Fly River', the afternoon bird is depicted as a creature whose call can draw a person's discontent or grievance to the surface. Muyu people claim the afternoon bird's song compels the listener to act on a matter that is held or buried in their heart. The meaning and affect of this bird's call depends on the listener's location in the moment. The song's lyrics in the Yonggom language centre around the Fly River which is an approximate eastern boundary of the region conceived as Muyu territory, and occasionally, homeland. In conversation, people talk about crossing the Fly in terms of 'going inside' and 'going outside'. The afternoon bird also delineates inside:outside. Flight has forced Muyu to live outside their own *dusun*, and it is a source of regret and grievance. The sound of the call of the afternoon bird reminds the listener of their *dusun* where the same call is heard. In the song, it is a yearning to return to this Muyu homeland that is assumed to be the matter buried in the heart of the exiled Muyu:

> On the edge of the Fly River
> I am sitting enjoying the mood of the afternoon
> The sun begins to set at the lower end of the Fly River
> A cluster of new clouds adorn the setting of the sun
> At the moment of enjoying, a voice is heard which is distressing
> The voice of the afternoon bird that ushers in the afternoon, its name afternoon bird
> Unsettles my inner thoughts
> That moment reminds me again of my homeland
> Where that matter makes me weep, it urges me to immediately free my Muyu homeland so that I might return.

Heard at East Awin, the afternoon bird's song invokes thoughts of a Muyu homeland, and when Muyu think of their homeland place such thoughts invoke the sound of the afternoon bird. Feld has described such a process as a 'doubly reciprocal motion': 'as place is sensed, senses are placed; as place makes sense, senses make place'.[2] That Muyu possess a 'sound world' is suggested by the invocatory powers of bird sound, and other soundful beings. The sound of the afternoon bird heard in Muyu camps at East Awin settlement does not effect a sense of familiarity there. Rather, familiar sounds evoke sentiments of loss at being outside.

Other insects and animals are also said to conjoin the Muyu and Awin regions in an ecological sense. Overlapping sounds can be disorienting as they locate the listener simultaneously in their garden or house at East Awin, and in their homeland *dusun*. For example, the glass-winged insect known as *enet* is found in both places, and its constant single pitch synchronises the two locations. At four o'clock, its call signals readiness for people working in their gardens to prepare to return home, at five, the call is repeated and signals the time for women to leave their work and return home carrying garden produce and children, and finally at six, the *enet*'s third call summons men to return home before the rainforest path becomes completely shadowed in darkness.

Shared seasons like the hatching of tortoises and ripening of breadfruit also synchronise and connect the Awin and Muyu regions. The tortoise season runs like this: in October/November, the hot season causes the lowering of the river's water level, and tortoises emerge to lay eggs on the river's sandy edge. In November/December, tortoise eggs begin to hatch. In January/February, the rainy season causes the river to rise and hatchlings swim away on their mother's back. The breadfruit season follows. In January, the breadfruit tree flowers. Between May and September, the secretion of *getah* or white sap indicates ripened breadfruit, and harvest commences. Yusuf had observed these seasons to be identical in both regions. The seasons of tortoise and breadfruit, synchronised from Samarai to Sorong (that is, the full length of New Guinea) constitute part of a discourse on New Guinea as a natural island. According to another elderly Muyu man named Viktor, birds that herald the hot and rainy seasons and times of daybreak and nightfall are present from east to west because of the island's form. Season is identified as a unifying feature of the entire island.

At East Awin, Muyu people are able to read familiar signs because the landscape remains subsumed under a single and familiar Muyu cosmology or scheme of explanation. The presence of birds and animals and other beings that are believed to possess powers of agency comparable to humans are central to Yonggom speakers' notions of place.[3] So birds in the Muyu and Awin regions signal the time of day by their calls and movements; the season by their consumption of ripening fruits; the weather by their presence or absence at particular times of the year; as well as misfortune and fortune. Predictions, warnings and indication of opportunities provide Muyu with 'critical social information'.[4]

The material above suggests that the Muyu homeland and East Awin both do, and do not, share a 'material essence' that might affiliate them as belonging to the same region.[5] The watershed *aknim* is physically located to the west of the international border, but some Muyu *dusun* extend across *aknim* and the international border, stretching as far as the western bank of the Ok Tedi in PNG. The *aknim* is mentioned by some Muyu as bounding Muyu territory, but the western and eastern banks of the Ok Tedi River are perhaps a more concrete threshold between Muyu and Awin regions. In the Muyu region, rivers as well as watersheds are fundamental to any delineation of the landscape. What can be said spatially at least, is that Muyu at East Awin find themselves on the far side of the *aknim* watershed, on the eastern banks of the Ok Tedi and Fly rivers, and on the eastern side of the international border. Species distribution and shared seasons aside, at East Awin, Muyu are 'outside' their territory in all of its spatial definitions.

According to Markus, a community health worker at East Awin who had once studied sociology at UNCEN, being outside causes him to feel destitute:

> Actually it is like we have all died, there is no feeling of being in a place. The body feels weightless. We are drifting. We appear busy enough here, eating and speaking, but we do not feel in a place. Our inner selves have been disturbed. Neither is it true that we are healthy. We are corpses, like dried bones without flesh or blood. But if we can return to the homeland, if there is freedom, our flesh and blood will return. It is as though our life force has been sapped. We don't feel sated. We feel awkward and exist in a constant state of hostility in relation to the landholders. We are vigilant and guarded, fearing repatriation by the government. In this place we are humiliated, trash, waste. Indeed, Indonesia has already killed me in an unseen manner by forcing me to flee my *dusun* and homeland.

The verb 'drifting' expresses inability to determine the direction of one's journey. Yusuf, Markus and other Muyu, described their flight into PNG in 1984, compelled or forced in a particular direction at a certain moment, and without time to settle affairs or gather possessions. Raids carried out by OPM fighters and Indonesian soldiers forced their flight. The activity of flight was not entirely spontaneous though. Muyu felt disenfranchised by the Indonesian government's failed promise of development. Extremely low rubber prices controlled by a rubber monopoly (IJ-JDF and its subsidiary P. T. Jodefo) deepened this sentiment among Muyu, and neighbouring Mandobo, Auyu and Mapi peoples.[6] Muyu felt themselves to be victims of deliberate and categorical neglect. In the early 1980s, the central government's development programs barely serviced the interior of Irian Jaya which contained 80 per cent of the population,[7] and military conflicts in rural areas further obstructed development activity.[8] But Muyu flight into PNG has also been attributed to 'unrequited reciprocity'.[9] Muyu did not speak of their treatment by Indonesians in terms of racism, cultural imperialism or ethnocide. Rather, they spoke about Indonesians' refusal to treat them as equals by establishing reciprocal relations.

The Catholic Church reported that between April 1984 and July 1985 around 9500 Muyu left their village and homes. Of these, about 2000 became internally displaced, and the remainder crossed the border into PNG. The exodus was distinct because of its size, and limited area of origin. Violence in this region catalogued by the Church documents a crescendo at the time of flight, over and above the usual pattern of Indonesian military and OPM attack and counter-attack.[10] By mid-1985, established villages in the Muyu region in Irian

Jaya were deserted, and only a small number of Muyu remained in the closest town of Mindiptana.

OPM supporters were said to have motivated Muyu to leave their villages, promising them a better future and a temporary stay in PNG. But the OPM also perpetrated acts of violence against some villagers. A Muyu woman at East Awin composed a song of lamentation that recalled retaliatory events between the Indonesian military and the OPM that led to the flight of her entire village into PNG in 1984. Known as a *tamagop*, the song contains a slow, laboured rhythm that can invoke weeping in the listener. It is subject to a repetitive cycle or round, its lines sung: 1/2/3, 2/3, 1/2/3. The song is titled 'You are strong, I am strong' and disguises the identity of the Indonesian military (referred to as 'you') and the OPM (referred to as 'I'). The songwriter aligns herself to the OPM, and not the Indonesian military which she positions as 'Other' by labelling it 'you':

1. We leave our place behind, we leave, all of us have left
2. Rain, rain, hungry all the journey
3. You are strong, I am strong caused us to leave our place behind and flee.

At East Awin, this lamentation was sung at the funerals of Muyu people. It was explained to me that the fighting drove people to flee, and indirectly caused their subsequent suffering and premature death at East Awin.

The physical, social and political circumstances of flight were also invoked in the naming of children. Naming allows the incorporation of individual experiences and incidences of flight into people's genealogies. Some Muyu children were given a second name drawn from the local language of the child's parents. It was this second name that sometimes mentioned displacement that made the circumstance of birth difficult. For example, in the Muyu language the name Mitikim refers to a child born in darkness during flight. Kiri or Kirikup signifies a child born during the journey of flight in 1984. Wangu-wangu is the name given to a child born in a temporary or transitory place. Kiriwain recalls unassisted birth in a place far from one's place of origin, and far from one's own parents. Benandim recalls the delivery of an infant onto bare ground without so much as material to wrap the child or a string bag in which to carry it. The mother of the girl child Benandim explained her choice of name: 'When people ask why this daughter has the name Benandim I will explain the destitute circumstances of her birth.' Benandim's mother imagined returning to her place of origin, and explaining to her kin and neighbours, her child's name and the circumstances of birth. Another child was given the name Octaviana, recalling her birth month October and birthplace: 'October was the month we shifted from the West Papuan side in the direction of Papua New Guinea.'

In some places entire villages fled, in others, only partial populations. Intact families and individuals fled. Some people crossed the border by taking familiar paths already marked by footprints that emerged at Yonggom villages on the eastern side of the border. Others took whatever path they could forge, and emerged randomly. People did not necessarily stay in the village of their arrival. Many travelled on to other villages where they had relatives. Some Muyu were received as kin by their fellow Yonggom speakers, others were not. Most squatted in makeshift camps alongside Yonggom villages on the eastern banks of the Fly River. (Anthropologist Stuart Kirsch used the term 'Yonggom' to refer to Yonggom-speaking Muyu as a tactic to counter the PNG government's perception of Muyu as foreigners in the period of refugee influx.[11]) The situation was further complicated by the fact that most Muyu wanted to return home. They remained in the border camps out of fear of punishment: from the OPM who wanted to retain a sizeable refugee enclave to attact world attention, and from the Indonesian military who claimed that the OPM had incited flight.

By mid-1987, about 1800 Muyu people had returned to Irian Jaya. Remaining Muyu in border camps were coaxed by the PNG government and UNHCR officials to relocate to East Awin. Despite the enticement of education, health services and rations by the UNHCR, and the severance of aid to border camps, the majority of Muyu people refused to relocate. Instead, they reorganised themselves into several large camps on the border. (In 2004, about 4500 Muyu refugees were living in 10 settlements spread over 150 kilometres in the border region of Western Province.[12]) Muyu at East Awin explained the refusal of their border counterparts to move as due to a desire to remain close to their *dusun*, the availability of sago on the border and links with local OPM groups. A history of feuding between Yonggom speakers and Awin was also alluded to:

> The [East Awin] location will give rise to problems between us and the Awin people there. We belong to different clans. Eventually such a situation would lead to war between the Yunggim [sic] and the Awin. Secondly, we have more means of making our livelihood than do the Awin. The Awin will become jealous of us. That will produce problems. Thirdly, the area in which we live is Yunggim territory. That's our clan territory—that's where we want to live. The Yunggim and the Awin are not compatible.[13]

Yonggom speakers on the PNG side were ambivalent about Muyu refugees. They wanted to help them due to their shared 'kinship and cultural affinity', yet they felt anger towards them for exhausting local resources, and feared their potential to cause illness and death through sorcery.[14] These sentiments are manifest in actions by Yonggom landowners towards Muyu refugees such as the disabling of water tanks, refusal to collaborate in joint initiatives like community schools, and refusal to allocate additional gardening land in spite of barrenness after 15 years of continuous cultivation.[15]

About 2500 Muyu people were eventually relocated to the UNHCR settlement at East Awin in 1987. It was an uncleared, unserviced site situated in the rainforest some 40 kilometres from the Fly River. At East Awin, the Awin landowners constituted part of the total social field in which Muyu conceived their displacement. Some Muyu felt themselves to be incarcerated at East Awin: bound by rules proscribing hunting activity, mobility and trading rights. Refugees generally were mindful of observing so-called 'landholder rules' at East Awin. None could elaborate how these rules were disseminated or policed however. Superficially at least, these rules appear to reflect a profane conservation ethic. But from a landholder viewpoint, the objects of these rules (sago, wild pigs, certain fish and prawns) are enspirited elements in a landscape. These so-called rules could also function—in the minds of Awin landholders and Muyu refugees—to mitigate the risk of 'desecrating' other people's land. Some Muyu elaborated their own rules for living in other people's *dusun* which were probably applicable in their own region in Irian Jaya. For example Yakub's list read:

1. Don't possess more than the landowner of that place.
2. Don't open a large garden.
3. Raise a little cash only for soap and salt.
4. Don't raise pigs for sale, only chickens.
5. Don't use dogs, guns, snares or traps in hunting.
6. Observe the boundary determined by the landowner.
7. Do nothing to disappoint the landowner.

Other rules mentioned use of the fish stupefying bomb called *tubah* made from tree-root, the sale of pig meat hunted outside the boundary, the raising of domesticated pigs and the cultivation of gardens. Two types of *tubah* were made and used at East Awin. One was made from the pounded root of a garden plant which was soaked in water and laid on the water's surface, making active fish dizzy but not affecting fish concealed in the mud floor. This type of *tubah* was allowed by the landowners, as was the use of goggles to spear prawns. However, *tubah* made from the grated root of a certain forest tree was proscribed. Laid on the surface of the water in the dry season when the river runs slowly, the grated root powder kills all fish beneath the surface. People using the grated root powder are meant to inform their downstream neighbours so that they might also gather fish from the water's surface. Refugees claimed that the landowners had prohibited use of this more potent *tubah* at East Awin. The use of *tubah* caused tensions between landowners and refugees, and among refugees themselves. For example, a Kanum woman told me that among her own people, *tubah* was only used where a person was very old and poor-sighted, and could not see or hold a hand-fishing line, and could not wait a long time for a catch. Only then could *tubah* be used, and only in a pool, isolated from the river flow.

Muyu at East Awin distinguished wild or forest pig from domestic pig. Tradition prescribed that wild pig meat ought not be sold, but eaten and shared among the hunter's neighbours. If a hunter used a spell or incantation to capture a wild pig and subsequently sold the meat, his spell's power would be diminished. Some refugees claimed there were Muyu hunters at East Awin who used a preventative spell enabling them to hunt and sell meat without consequence. In an incident in the marketplace at East Awin in 1995, a landowner announced that the sale of wild meat by refugees was prohibited. Wild meat included pig, kangaroo, cassowary, large fish including catfish, and tortoise. According to the Muyu narrator, because little game remained inside the East Awin boundary, it was assumed that any game sold in the market had probably been hunted outside the camp boundary. According to Yakub, landholders routinely inspected meat sold in the market at East Awin, querying: 'Where was that animal hunted?' In 1999, a landholder made a public announcement in the East Awin marketplace that refugees could not sell wild pig meat for more than three kina (in 2000, 1PGK = approx. $US0.4). It was explained that while refugees hunted pigs with their own effort—according them some right of benefit—landholders resented being asked to pay high prices for wild pig grown on their land.

While Muyu possessed their own houses and restricted gardening plots at East Awin, there was no expanse of uncultivated hunting ground or sago forest. Markus explained to me that Muyu farmers felt oppressed living in such a state:

> We do not feel free. Our own place is divided into *dusun*, and each *dusun* has a boundary that is not crossed arbitrarily. Hunting on land, sea, river has a boundary limit, but life inside one's *dusun* is unhindered. Living here in another people's place is difficult. The place is still dominated, controlled by the owners who have divided the place into areas. Here, we live inside a gardening plot.

Constricted space caused particular tensions about raising pigs. One camp allowed their pigs to roam freely and they constantly caused damage to the neighbouring camp's gardens. Warnings and reprisals always followed. When sickness occurred in the pig owner's village, the garden owners were blamed, for it was known that they held a pre-existing grievance. When a pig is caught inside a person's garden it may be killed. If the garden owner is angry he may sell the meat, but if he is a reasonable man he will divide the meat with the pig's owner. The killing of a pig to avenge a damaged garden installs another layer of grievance. Roaming pigs caused other problems. Chickens were eaten by pigs, and young pigs were eaten by domestic dogs. According to a Muyu man whose garden had been destroyed on several occasions by pigs from the neighbouring Dani camp, all of these incidents were a result of space which was both constrained and undefined at East Awin.

Stabling pigs inside camps at East Awin settlement meant the owners were compelled to cart large quantities of cassava from distant gardens, and water from distant streams in order to tend the pigs. In 1996, Muyu people from Atkamba camp collectively fenced an open area inside the camp so that pigs could roam an enclosed space. The fence was completed, but the effort required to cart cassava from distant gardens proved too labour intensive and the project folded. The East Awin administration eventually prohibited the raising of pigs inside the camps. Police distributed notices to each camp outlining the prohibition due to disease risks caused by pigs defecating on village paths, and disputes caused by damaged gardens. Penning pigs in gardens located far from the residential camp was not without difficulty either, as owners were required to make the journey to the garden several times a day for feeding and watering.

Rules relating to cultivation were broadcast from the pulpit by Catholic Church elders to the Muyu congregation. They advised about economical use of garden land:

1. Gardens should not be too large.
2. New gardens should be opened only after the previous one is barren.
3. Forest should not be cleared too early because left uncultivated it will rapidly become barren, reverting to undergrowth. If cleared again it will become blade *kunai* grassland.
4. Uncleared forest should be conserved for gathering timber for building, firewood and rattan.

Less effort was required to open a new garden than to re-clear land that had reverted to *kunai* grassland. Over-zealous clearing produced quarrels among refugee neighbours. Gardeners who had determined their boundaries but not yet cleared the entire space, often found the unoccupied area appropriated by their neighbours. Outward expansion meant that people were forced to walk longer and longer distances to gather firewood, and to attend their gardens. Building materials such as rattan, hardwood for foundation posts, and *nibung* palm for flooring and walls, became scarce inside the settlement boundary and people were forced to seek these materials outside. In theory they were meant to compensate the landholders for anything gathered outside. According to Markus, many people assumed that because they would return to their own *dusun* there was no need to adapt their cultivation practice to the situation at East Awin. But Markus warned against this malaise. He believed that conversion of forest to grassland inside the East Awin boundary could eventually cause famine.

Muyu maintained their connection with their original *dusun*. From East Awin, fathers mapped *dusun* in order to familiarise sons born or raised outside, and they named children in a way that identified their *dusun* rights. Each of these practices anticipated eventual return. Markus had articulated the boundaries, topography and history of his *dusun* to his son Theo:

> I drew a map of my *dusun* for my youngest son. I carried him here [to PNG] as a small child in 1984. He has no recollection of his *dusun*. I explained to him the name of the *dusun*, the watersheds, the rivers and sago swamp. I told him places with other names that he must not disturb because these are owned by someone else. I told him about the places of *kenari* trees and three deep river pools. I told him where his own share lies in relation to his brothers inside of the family *dusun*. I advised him that there is no point in making a garden on the hilly part as the low-lying ground is the most fertile and can grow rice paddy and mung beans. I told him of the forbidden places above a waterfall. If he goes to that place he may be cursed, that place will not ever bring fortune and will bring barrenness and sickness.

Markus said that when his son Theo was mature enough to visit his father's *dusun* in Irian Jaya, Markus would advise him to speak with neighbours about their *dusun* boundaries. Then Markus would quiz Theo about the neighbours' assertions, and confirm or dispute their claims.

According to Markus, a dying man at East Awin ought to counsel his sons about the division of his property. First, he should advise his sons not to seize another's land, but to work together and avoid conflict. Second, he should reiterate the boundaries of his *dusun*, and the boundaries of each son's portion. Finally, he should map these boundaries mindful of his sons' lack of familiarity with his *dusun*:

> When the time comes for us to stand alone we will be compelled to return. We only arrived here. But my origin is over there, the land of my parents and their parents and their parents; the land of my forefathers. Gardens have been planted and bequeathed over and over. This is the foundation upon which my own sons will return. It must be pointed out to them—these are your orchards of perennial trees: sago, rubber, rambutan, coconut, breadfruit, matoa, *ketapang*, *kenari*, pandanus, *areca* nut, rose-apple and mango. All of these were planted by your own grandparents. This is your wealth and property.

Some Muyu refugees had appointed *dusun* caretakers who were accorded certain rights of use. Other families had sent individual members from East Awin back to Irian Jaya to look after their *dusun*. Since 1984 when Yakub's entire village fled into PNG, villagers had installed caretakers on *dusun* that faced the main

Waropko–Mindiptana Road. On behalf of absent owners, caretakers had fixed stakes along the road's edge and built bush houses visible from the road so that the land appeared to be occupied. The Indonesian government considered Yakub's area to be an optimum transmigration location as it comprised riverflat country: its dark, fertile soil was ideal for cultivating rice, peanuts and fruits. Installing a caretaker was a pragmatic arrangement. One man claimed that if he did not allow right of use or right of care to a male relative living within walking distance of his *dusun*, then it would revert to overgrown forest. This man allowed his relative to fell sago on the condition that he cleared the area so that a replacement sucker would grow.

Depending on the circumstances, absence from one's *dusun* could also diminish a person's claim to ownership. Yakub used the metaphor of 'thinning' to describe the effect of absence on ownership. Inversely, a caretaker's rights could increase with the passing of time, and he may be reluctant to relinquish his rights in the event of the landholder's return. Among Muyu, distribution of land rights to non-relatives was flexible, and in the instance of land surplus, usufruct or right of use may be granted to a friend, affine or person from another area. Continued use of land may effect full ownership, but it was more likely that full ownership and lineage membership would be installed in their descendants.[16] A returning Muyu landholder had lost rights over his ancestral *dusun* because he had been unsuccessful in reasserting his authority over the caretaker. The relation between caretaker and landholder could also get caught up in political manoeuvring. I heard the story at East Awin of a Muyu refugee who returned to his *dusun* and proceeded to re-establish his full rights of ownership. The caretaker had reacted by reporting the returnee to the Indonesian military, claiming him to be an OPM member.

Muyu experience of displacement on Awin land is not diminished because of their proximity to their homeland, quite the contrary. From East Awin, Muyu people represent their territory as the western horizon, as though there is nothing further west than Muyu territory. Whenever I was in the company of a Muyu person at sunset or dusk, he or she would gesture in the westward direction of the setting sun with great sadness: 'O! See how the sun is setting in our place over there.' Markus told me that at sunset he usually wept a little: 'It is not just me, it is everyone here. I ask myself: "Why until now have we remained so long in the rainforest when there is no sentiment to stay?" We came to live here without the slightest desire. We are just waiting.'

ENDNOTES

[1] Herlihy in Blaskett, p. 53.

[2] Stephen Feld, 'Waterfalls of song: an acoustemology of place resounding in Bosavi, Papua New Guinea', in S. Feld and K. H. Basso (eds), *Senses of place*, School of American Research Press, Santa Fe, New Mexico, p. 91.

[3] Kirsch, 'Changing views.'

[4] Kirsch, 'Changing views'.

[5] Casey, 'How to get from space to place in a fairly short stretch of time: phenomenological prolegomena', in S. Feld and K. Basso, p. 30.

[6] George Aditjondro, 'The Irian Jaya refugee and returnee problem: a state-of-the-art report and options for the future', unpublished report.

[7] Blaskett, p. 172.

[8] Manning and Rumbiak, p. 108.

[9] Kirsch, 'Refugees and representations: politics, critical discourse and ethnography along the New Guinea border', in M. Morgan and S. Leggett (eds) *Mainstream(s) and margins: cultural politics in the '90s*, Greenwood Press, Connecticut, p. 226.

[10] Jayapura Secretartiat of Peace and Justice, 'Situational report on returnees from Papua New Guinea to Irian Jaya dealing in particular with returnees to the Waropko-Mindiptana area', 1998.

[11] Stuart Kirsch, pers. comm.

[12] Jacques Gros, pers. comm.

[13] ICJ, *Status of border crossers*, p. 51.

[14] Kirsch, 'The Yonggom of New Guinea', pp. 53–4.

[15] S. Lutz and H. Hansen, 'OED social programme for refugees in the Western Province', unpublished report.

[16] Kirsch, *The Yonggom of New Guinea*, p 15.

Chapter 5

Refugee settlements as social spaces

On Saturday afternoons, women sellers spread their produce on empty 10-kilogram rice bags outside the Saint Bertilla Catholic Church, located at the opening of Atkamba camp at East Awin. They offered fresh pig meat cut into portions, smoked *couscous* carcass, raw and cooked *gomo* nuts from the breadfruit tree, unshelled peanuts tied by their stalks into bunches, red chillis and ginger, taro, cassava and sweet potato, a variety of greens, a dozen types of banana, pineapples and *soursop*. On one particular Saturday while stopping to buy eggs from a seller, I found myself standing next to Cecilia. She introduced the egg seller to me as Angelina, her daughter's grandmother. That is, Angelina the seller was Cecilia's own mother. I had spent a lot of time with Cecilia cooking and eating, but she had never mentioned her 'mama' Angelina, and I had never met her. But most curious was the fact that Angelina appeared to be about the same age as Cecilia herself—about thirty-five years old. When I queried her, she explained that Angelina's face, stature and body movement resembled those of Cecilia's mother in 1992: 'Mama appears as my own mother did when I last saw her.' Cecilia's daughter called Angelina 'Nenek' or grandmother, and sometimes Angelina's daughter stayed with Cecilia. The relationship between the women was signified by exchange. At the market, Cecilia—who received wages as a teacher—always purchased vegetables from Angelina. She paid with high denomination coins, and refused change. Angelina sometimes gave Cecilia a billum or string bag laden with produce from her own extensive garden. When Cecilia occasionally bought bulk rice from town, she gave Angelina several kilos. Rice was a luxury item at East Awin, and most people could only afford to buy salt, and occasionally peanut oil to supplement their diet of sweet potato, bananas and greens.

Cecilia and Angelina have generated a kind of 'fictive kinship': a relationship formed out of Angelina's physical resemblance to Cecilia's mother. The name that West Papuans give to this practice is *tukar muka* which means literally 'exchanging faces'. Leonardo, whose fictive kinship is elaborated below, explained the practice: 'I see that person living close to me in the same way as I see the one living far.' Exchanging faces is not specific to the condition of exile. It may be practised when a person experiences the absence of a close relative due to death, or if they are outside their place of origin. A fictive kin relation may be more enduring than the relation with the absent person, and may continue after the return of the absent relative. Leonardo outlined the process of exchanging faces. If by chance a person meets someone whose physical appearance resembles an absent or deceased relative, they may approach that person and invite them to take on the role of the absent relative. Next they will invite the person to eat, perhaps offering small gifts before revealing their intention: 'I see you the same as X. I want to take you as X.' It may be a moment of intense emotion. At East Awin, exchanging faces was described as something many practised, recognised by most people and possessing a reciprocal or exchange character. If a person accepts another's identification of them, both assume the obligations of their respective roles. For example, a woman recognising a man as her maternal uncle will assume the role of his niece.

Leonardo saw the features of his deceased younger sister in his neighbour Sofia. After exchanging faces, Leonardo used 'younger sister' to address Sofia, and 'brother-in-law' to address Sofia's husband. In return, Sofia called Leonardo 'older brother', and her children addressed him as 'maternal uncle'. Leonardo's identification of Sofia as his deceased younger sister, and Sofia's acceptance of this role meant that they held expectations of one another as siblings. As his sister's brother, Leonardo had also taken on the responsibility of maternal uncle to Sofia's children. Among Muyu and north coast and island West Papuans, the maternal uncle receives bride-price payment for his sister, and contributes to the bride-price payments for his sister's sons, although both of these exchanges may involve several other contributors and recipients. At East Awin, the role of maternal uncle could also be approximated pragmatically, that is, without attention to physical resemblance. For example, one man's bride-price was provided by his father's sister and her husband in the absence of other relatives at East Awin. In Irian Jaya, the payment was acknowledged by the man's parents and uncles who then returned the payment to relatives of the paternal aunt.

The practice of exchanging faces at East Awin creates ties between non-kin in the same and different camps. Appadurai's theorising of locality further extends an explanation of the effect of fictive kinship.[1] East Awin is a social formation where families (excepting Muyu) tend to be nuclear, because only the able-bodied could flee. In a situation where previously extended families are no longer intact, people may intentionally or incidentally establish fictive kinship. The formation of these relations creates a new social space which may in turn generate other social spaces, as the relation between the two individuals extends into their respective kin, neighbour and enemy groupings. Through Angelina, Cecilia has entrée into Atkamba camp, and vice versa, which generates contexts for new social spaces.

The production of 'new social spaces' is central to Appadurai's thesis of 'locality'.[2] Locality resembles the sentiment of 'home' in that it describes the dimension of sociality between people. But it is the way Appadurai theorises the production of locality and what locality generates, that is distinctive. East Awin settlement can be described as a refugee grouping produced by the policy and actions of the PNG government and UNHCR. The relocation of 4000 people to a small area in a short space of time compelled relationality as people settled themselves among others, and participated in intersecting fraternities as parents of school children, members of church congregations and Bible-reading groups, sellers or buyers in the market, patients at clinics, users of public paths, etc. The production of 'locality' can be encouraged. The establishment of five primary schools in particular locations in the settlement, compulsory enrolment of children in the school catchment, and requirement for each school to form parent representative bodies, produced a context which compelled parents to form committees. In and through this association and its fetes and civic events, opportunities for other social spaces came to be generated.

Configuration of the settlement was historical—in most cases, the camp population and camp name had simply been transplanted to East Awin from its previous location on the border. Because entire villages had fled, intact families across three generations were not uncommon in Muyu camps at East Awin. But separation had occurred in many instances where elderly and frail parents were left behind, or had returned to their *dusun* in Irian Jaya. The territorial and genealogical basis of the nine Muyu camps at East Awin contrasted other camps. Most northerners at East Awin were urban dwellers who had fled as individuals or nuclear family groups from the coastal towns of Sorong, Manokwari, Serui, Biak and Jayapura. Luther claimed that his own northerner camp Waraston functioned as a community by virtue of residents' 'urban disposition'. By this he meant that in the absence of kin, genealogically unrelated neighbours acted towards each other as kin. At Waraston, illness or death was handled by a person's neighbours and the camp generally. Alliances between northerners were initially established in the first border camp at Vanimo, where groups coalesced around two leaders from the islands of Biak and Serui. When these two groups relocated to East Awin, they were initially resettled by the administration in camps located 25 kilometres apart. Luther reckoned that the location of the camps had been predetermined by the camp administration to be at opposite ends to prevent any prospect of solidarity, thereby weakening the struggle. For his part, Luther categorised all northerners as family regardless of their politics: shared origin was more important than political persuasion.

Camps at East Awin comprised people who shared places of origin, and/or membership of the same political or religious group. Outside these alliances distrust tended to prevail. Some people's trust only extended to their immediate family. Behaviour in relation to mail is illustrative. Most people at East Awin expressed a preference for renting a post office box of their own in the distant town of Kiunga. By distant I mean that it could take at least 12 hours to navigate the rainforest path and river crossing from East Awin to Kiunga. The second-best option was to use the post office box of one's church at East Awin, or the address of a relative living in Kiunga. The least reliable option was to send and receive mail through the camp administration's public post box, as people claimed that mail was pilfered and were reluctant to entrust the collection of their mail to anyone else. Back in Canberra I received letters from people anxiously inquiring whether I had received their mail, or whether I had sent mail that they had not received.

Muyu avoided involving themselves in business with their own clan. Rather, they preferred to ally themselves with those whose village origin was the same, but whose clan was different. None of the kiosks at East Awin were owned or operated by Muyu. According to Markus, this was because Muyu feared social envy.[3] Some claimed refugeeness as an economic condition to be shared by all. Wage-earning Muyu, such as teachers or nurses, contrasted with other Muyu toiling in their gardens for a few lousy *toea*. Markus, a teacher, tried to remedy this imbalance by purchasing produce from Muyu sellers in the market despite his own extensive garden, and fulfilling requests for assistance whenever he was able.

Solidarity between Muyu refugees was based on their camp of residence at East Awin. The following incident, which occurred in the St Bertilla market at the entrance to Atkamba camp, demonstrates alliance among some Muyu based on perceived inequality. A prominent Muyu woman from Atkamba announced in the market one Saturday that women from other camps at East Awin were no longer welcome to sell their produce at St Bertilla market. Women from other camps (including Muyu camps), whose gardens were located in the vicinity of larger rivers, were able to grow large vegetables and irrigated varieties: cucumbers, broad-leafed *kangkung*, chives and snake beans. The incidental location of their gardens was providing this group with a competitive advantage over the Atkamba sellers whose gardening land was dry.

Other sellers in the market experienced exclusion for different reasons. Twelve months after Cecilia's arrival at East Awin with 100 other families from Sota, only six families remained. In the following year, Cecilia's husband also left for Irian Jaya to see for himself the fate of refugees who had returned. Explaining her sense of abandonment at this time, Cecilia used a phrase which ordinarily describes a child abandoned by its parents, or if a person has no surviving relatives:

> We felt left behind like abandoned children when we recalled those people who had already returned, and at other times when there were disputes with the neighbouring camp at East Awin. We were now a very small camp and felt threatened, enclosed. So we tried not to make trouble, preferring instead to yield to others' demands. We adopted an attitude of *nai sepne* which in our language means 'just leave it'.

Cecilia's experience of living at East Awin was affected by the size of her camp in relation to neighbouring camps. It was the perception of minority that was the basis of her camp's solidarity, and their acquiescence:

> When we first arrived, [we] baked cassava cakes to sell in the [East Awin] market. Because the cakes were enticing, other vendors protested that buyers were spending all of their money on our cakes and they were taking home their produce unsold. Then some of these other women copied our cakes, but buyers still bought from us and those women took their cakes home, unsold. They protested again and we thought: better we stop selling cakes than have this bitterness between us—we are only a few people here.

Northerner leaders at Waraston camp understood and promoted activities of community formation and solidarity. At their previous border camp near Vanimo, they had established a co-operative and purchased an outboard motor for fishing. At East Awin, their business operations included a passenger/freight truck operating between East Awin and the Fly River, and a motorised canoe operating between the Fly River ramp and the town of Kiunga. Profits from the truck and canoe were managed by the 'Committee for Community Prosperity'. They funded camp activities such as catering at commemorative flag-raising ceremonies, and seed grants for women's groups and family-based enterprises. These funds also supported administration (post, phone, transport) related to political business.

Everyday activity and interaction within and across camps generated a social space/s from which departure was considered as homeparting. Departures meant parting from a place where one had experienced social belonging. Casey has described the way that a place gathers things in its midst: experiences, thoughts, histories, as well as animate and inanimate entities.[4] Repatriation of friends and relatives was viewed with disappointment, for their return was considered premature. It was also seen as the loss of loved ones from a familiar place they had shared. The song below, titled 'It's said you want to leave', recalls a person learning of the imminent departure of another, and imagines everyday life at East Awin in that person's absence. Time and place are disrupted, rendered suddenly dark by the loss. The song approaches East Awin uniquely as a homeplace from where parting occurs:

> *First verse*: It's said you want to leave
> The sun will go down
> When your face no longer radiates
> Our village will become dark.

> *Second verse*: Until now you have not yet said
> Don't understand the pounding of my heart
> I will wait faithfully

Until your news arrives.

Chorus: Let's sit for a moment and talk
You can't leave in a rush
Don't forget the valley of East Awin
And a certain person and their affection.

To leave East Awin after burying someone close was to leave behind traces of that person's productive activity such as their garden. In the period following death, places associated with the deceased may be the subject of avoidance for Muyu, as features of the landscape 'resonate with events from the life of the deceased'.[5] Repatriation to Irian Jaya meant that the graves of deceased family members at East Awin would be left derelict. Burial of family members established an enduring connection with a place previously considered both foreign and temporary. Burial made refugees' relation to East Awin ambiguous.

A PNG government regulation prescribed the public cemetery at East Awin as the official place of burial. In the past, the camp administration had provided transport of the coffin from the deceased person's home to the cemetery. But since the decline of government services, relatives had begun to bury their dead nearby: next to their houses, and on the perimeter of churches. I was told: 'Here, everyone is determined in spite of the consequences to bury their dead beside their house. If the deceased is beloved, the person's family will not permit the grave to be far from their house.' People were reluctant to bury the dead in the public cemetery because rumours circulated that pigs from the neighbouring camp roamed freely, and rooted out fresh burial sites. It was also pragmatic to bury nearby. The cemetery was too far to carry a coffin if there was no transport, and a nearby grave was more readily cared for, and more easily identifiable in the event of exhumation.

The prospect of leaving a deceased relative behind in a distant place like East Awin made people anxious. They talked about how to bury bodies in order to recover them easily. Some spoke of exhuming bones for reburial in a patriot's cemetery. In the event of *merdeka*, people would exhume the graves of 'important people' at East Awin, re-interring them in their place of origin. Leonardo cited a book about a Vietnam war memorial in the United States (US) that gave a complete history of those buried: name, rank, date and cause of death. He proposed that the bones of West Papuan patriots killed on the border should be recovered: 'Bones or ashes, it is important that their families see the remains with their own eyes.' For those graves not exhumed, relatives would install durable signs like a cement surface or tin roof, or prominent trees like coconut, *ketapang* and breadfruit. These things would identify the grave to descendants. The rationale was that: 'Parents must not disappear or be finished, their graves must be known by their grandchildren.' Some claimed that as the site of burial was not their land, graves were vulnerable to tampering and bones could be removed. Some feared the forest would become overgrown, concealing the cemetery completely. When Yakub's adult son drowned tragically in the Fly River, he buried him at Kiunga, which he considered to be more proximate to his *dusun* in Irian Jaya than East Awin. Yakub planned that in the event of his repatriation he could readily attend his son's grave in Kiunga.

Burial of West Papuan children born in PNG caused particular sadness because it was considered that they had never seen their actual place of origin. The death of an adult person was mourned because they would not see their beloved homeland again. At the funeral of Lina—whose life is recounted in Chapter 11—mourners sang songs lamenting her premature departure. In a lamentation song, the elderly Mamberamo singer regretted that she and Lina would not retrace the journey home together: 'Together we came to this place / O you have left us before we could return home / You have abandoned us in this foreign place which is not ours.'

The precariousness of exile where one may live and die alone is epitomised in the story of the death of Leonardo's uncle in an Amsterdam apartment. By the time his uncle's body was discovered, it had decomposed, and the odour of the putrefied body had permeated the apartment. People recounting this story expressed horror that someone could die in an urban setting and remain undiscovered for a long period of time. Leonardo's uncle was neither washed, dressed, watched over nor lamented. The imperative of burial in the homeland was recalled in stories told of elderly West Papuans living in exile in the Netherlands. One man wrote a letter to Indonesia's President Habibie about his desire to return to West Papua to die. The letter recalled the two places of West Papuan and Holland metaphorically, in terms of objects deemed native to each: '[When] I die, [better to be] buried beneath a coconut palm than an apple tree.' The meaning of the place of burial illuminates the notion of home. Lovell has written that for people exhumed and reburied after a period of 'mortuary exile', as well as people returning from exile in order to die and be buried in their home village, home is conceived as a place of return, 'an original settlement where peace can finally be found and experienced, even after death'.[6]

At East Awin also, people were compelled to bring their deceased kin out of mortuary exile. On return to the homeland or the original settlement, the experience of peace would be affected by the memory of deceased kin left behind in the place of exile. In spite of the generation of East Awin as a social space—even a homeplace from where parting occurred—most people aspired to return to their geographical place of origin. As long as the deceased could be repatriated, people believed that true peace could only be had in the homeland—for the living and the dead.

ENDNOTES

[1] Appadurai

[2] Appadurai, pp. 178–99.

[3] cf. Pim Schoorl, *Kebudayaan dan Perubahan Suku Muyu dalam Arus Modernisasi Irian Jaya,* Grasindo, Jakarta, 1997, p. 25.

[4] Casey, 'How to get from space', pp. 24–5.

[5] Kirsch, 'The Yonggom of New Guinea', pp. 125–6.

[6] N. Lovell, 'Introduction: belonging in need of emplacement?', in N. Lovell (ed.), *Locality and belonging,* Routledge, London, 1998, p. 3.

Chapter 6

Inscribing the empty rainforest with our history

Cutting through the coarse outer skin of the pineapple, Regina scored the eyes until the flesh was smooth. Juice coursed down the knife blade dripping though the slatted floor to the dusty ground below. She passed the pineapple on a tin plate and sat beside me on the floor, eyeing me keenly. Then she apologised for the taste of the pineapple, it was neither sweet nor fragrant compared to those grown in her own *dusun*. Cucumbers and bananas were also without aroma. Regina told me that in her own place, she could not open the skin of a baked banana without the intense aroma being discerned by others. At East Awin, cucumbers and bananas were not like those fruits of the same name that they had cultivated in their own place. It was much the same with Regina's house at East Awin. It was the sort of building in which she would have previously stored *kumbile* tubers—it was not fit for habitation.[1]

Regina had 15 children, and most of her daughters lived with her at East Awin. Her husband and sons had returned to Irian Jaya not long after the family's arrival in 1992. It was said that they could not bear living on tinned mackerel and rice alone. Their appetites never sated, they chose to return to their own region in spite of the dangers. The *dusun* surrounding Regina's village was abundant with deer, fish, coconut and sago. It lay in a border region where both West Papuan freedom fighters and Indonesian soldiers moved. At East Awin, Regina had constructed three houses, each one salvaged from the former. Timber foundation posts and sago thatch were purchased with money received in a bride-price payment from Regina's son-in-law, a labourer in the local Ok Tedi copper mine. Each of Regina's houses had been better than the last. But even the most recent was nothing like the house she had been forced to abandon. Her deprivation at East Awin served to remind her of previous comfort.

My first visit to Regina's house commenced with a barrage of apology. Shortage of building materials meant she had been unable to set aside a room to receive visitors. She wanted to be able to offer a chair to sit on, and a table to eat at. Chairs and tables guarded against disorder, and to eat at a table was to eat in a 'civilised' manner. Regina expressed shame at hosting a visitor in such a place. Then she proceeded to list the qualities of the house she had lived in before fleeing. It had a tin roof, cement walls, electricity and running water, and had been built by a tradesperson. On their arrival at East Awin, she and her daughters had been obliged to sleep 'precisely like animals: there were no walls'. They learned to build their own house, but these houses were not houses in which 'to really live'. Rather, they resembled the sort of space in which Regina had previously stored the *kumbile* tuber. 'We don't choose to live like this,' she told me. Yet, Regina and her daughters were able to reflect that, unlike other refugees in the world whom they had read about in UNHCR magazines in the school library, and who were penned like animals, West Papuans were permitted to choose a site and design and build their own houses at East Awin. They understood their relative fortune.

Some limits had been placed on refugee housing at East Awin. A plan to kiln-fire clay bricks was obstructed. According to a Muyu man who helped make the bricks, the settlement administrator prohibited the plan on the grounds that refugees were not permitted to build ostentatious houses, and must live in bush houses like the Awin landholders. His rationale was about equality: refugees must not appear to be privileged, or live differently to the local landholders. Houses at East Awin were characterised by their bricolage quality, made from whatever material was available. Shortage of building materials such as timber meant that many Muyu houses at East Awin were less substantial than the owner's previous dwelling in the border camps where bush material was plentiful. One woman complained that she and her husband and two young children were forced to occupy one end of her father's house, because there was not enough roofing material to build a separate house. The general rule of residence at East Awin was virilocal, that is, women shifted to the same camp and/or household as their husband's parents. It had happened that a man had resided in the house of his wife's family when they were from the same camp, but no man had shifted to his wife's family's home in another camp.

House size reflected the owner's perception of the future. Initially on their arrival at East Awin, refugees had co-operatively built rectangular dormitories on the edge of camps. Then they had each constructed their own houses. Many times I heard: 'We did not need very big houses because we were mid-journey.' A house that was considered elaborate boasted a tin roof rather than sago thatch, and milled timber walls and flooring rather than adzed bush timber. Among Muyu people, such a house could invoke the envy of others. The risks are expressed in the aphorism: 'A new house means you're just looking to die.' According to Markus, anything that differentiates a Muyu person from their neighbour is likely to draw the attention and envy of others. One needed to keep up the appearance of ordinariness by living in a house made from bush materials, wearing shabby clothes, not revealing cash in public, and not disclosing details of compensation or bride-price payments. Markus characterised Muyu people as wary, a disposition so naturalised that there is no word in the Yonggom language to describe it. The word '*katkile*' is used to warn someone to be especially cautious to avoid causing envy or grievance in others.

Tensions existed at East Awin because everyone experienced shortage at some time, and was compelled to borrow from someone else. If a Muyu person borrows or requests something, they may become the subject of conversation and mockery later. Money is a particularly fraught thing to borrow. If too much time lapses before a person repays a loan, the borrower is vulnerable because the loan-giver will feel aggrieved. Many Muyu people had shifted outside their original camps that had become crowded to establish houses on vacant land along the edge of the main road into East Awin. This was because dense settlement increased people's interaction, and increased the risk of being misunderstood or misrepresented. Among Muyu, such a situation easily led to dispute and the accusation of sorcery.

Sorcery may be performed using a departed person's belongings. Regina explained that when her family eventually returned home to Irian Jaya they would gather their traces and old things for burning: 'Otherwise the unknown contents of a person's heart may cause trouble.' Underlying Regina's statement is the conviction that enmities that appear dormant eventually come to the surface. A new house could be surrendered to another family, but an older house ought to be burned. There were two reasons for this. First, a house becomes the most tangible trace of a person, and can be readily used for sorcery if abandoned intact. Second, a metaphysical relationship can be established between a dwelling and the occupants, and new occupants are at risk of being disturbed by the guardian spirit of the former residents. A guardian spirit may continue to occupy an empty house to dissuade intruders.

Regardless of origin, refugees at East Awin related the destruction of a house to destruction of the body or self. The analogous relation between dwellings and bodies is almost inevitable given the: 'intimate relationship between the human body and the dwellings in which it is placed (and where it places itself)'.[2] Muyu people conceive the kitchen hearth as the navel or centre of the house, where everything of value arrives. In a Muyu practice to mark the occupation of a new house, the hearth is set, lit for the first time, and celebrated as the source of life in the new house. A shaman or *dukun* prays that such things as game, garden produce and cash will be drawn to the hearth of the new house, and procured quickly and successfully. The *dukun* also requests that the new dwelling be kept warm, and manifest good fortune and prosperity. A church elder may install a ladder or steps to the house with a prayer requesting that many visitors enter and exit by way of the new steps. Like the *dukun*, the church elder blesses the hearth, seeking God's protection of the occupants, and guarding against the house becoming cold or disaffected. Muyu perception of states of warmth and cold in the house are said to be associated with the death of a woman figure like a mother, and the loss of her nurturing presence.[3]

A 'dwelling place' is defined by Casey as a place that must possess 'a certain felt familiarity'.[4] Familiarity is about ambience and structure rather than time of occupation or acquaintance. So a dwelling place becomes a *kind* of dwelling rather than a particular building.[5] By way of example, at the front entrance to his house at East Awin, Markus had installed steps carved in semi-circular fashion out of a tree trunk. Referred to as *kum*, he described the steps in terms of familiarity, they were 'the ancestral tradition of his Muyu tribe'. *Kum* requires a particular stepping motion that engages the entire body: the toes, ankles, knees, hips, fingers, wrists, elbows and shoulders. The action of ascending and descending *kum* at East Awin produces familiarity in Muyu refugees. Casey proposes that 'inhabiting' is an activity that is dependent on the body, and bodily movement. In residing, the body is an agent of habit memories that are formed over a period of time, and these memories are recalled through the re-enactment of bodily motions.[6] Familiarity created by 'habitual body memories' allows people to orient themselves in a new place or residence. Muyu people at East Awin commented that they had adjusted to cooking over a hearth set into the floor, rather than the hip-level standing hearth that they were accustomed to. Similarly, they had adjusted to a hearth, and cooking activity, located in the middle of the house, rather than in a separate space. This adaptation was necessary because there was no sago at East Awin, and people cured alternative roof thatching with hearth smoke to increase its durability.

Old houses made of organic bush materials decomposed over time in the tropical climate. From these bush materials precious little could be retrieved or sold. Houses built from manufactured materials were dismantled or sold intact. Tin and milled timber fetched almost new prices at East Awin because of the convenience of on-site removal. Departing residents commonly sold their houses to neighbours, or houses were sold and dismantled for the extension of an existing house, or a new building. Some houses were gifted to relatives or friends at the time of the owner's departure. The practices of selling, gifting and renovating houses reflects people's conception of their house and garden at East Awin as their own property. Houses and gardens were conceived as refugee property in spite of the fact that these houses were located on land that, according to the owners, had not been fully compensated. This apparent anomaly was explained by Markus:

> Although this is not my place and I hold rights of use only, my house is considered my own property. It can be sold: it is an object of value. According to land regulations, it cannot be sold. But if I return home or shift to another place I may sell my house or new garden to compensate my building materials and labour. The payment may be in-kind, not necessarily cash.

Refugees had built houses and gardens with their own labour, in a place that they had judged to be 'empty' upon their arrival. Neither camp nor garden areas had been cleared. They recalled their initial impressions of East Awin as wilderness which was both empty and engulfing. The rainforest was dense and crawling with snakes. Giant cockroaches scuttled about in the night and chewed the fingers—smelling of tinned fish—of sleeping children and adults. Needle-thorned plants had to be cleared. Extraordinary wind gusts tore off house roofs as they were laid, and coated tin dishes with dust. The irony of a dense rainforest being labelled 'empty' contains its own logic.[7] For it is from the standpoint of a sedentary gardener that an uncultivated site can be labelled empty. Both Muyu refugees and Awin landholders are shifting cultivators, but it happened that the landholders had only sparsely settled East Awin before 1987. For Muyu, a place that is not empty is an occupied place or *dusun*, marked by habitation and cultivation and containing memories and histories.[8] By extension, empty refers to the absence of features that make the landscape meaningful and productive for Muyu. Markus explained: 'When we arrived here, there was not a single sago tree, cassava plant, breadfruit tree or banana palm. If the land was truly owned, the old people would have planted long-living trees.' Naturally for the landholders, East Awin was both centrally located and entirely meaningful: it was their ancestral place.

The notion of space as empty is a fairly conventional response to any new space that is not the person's own space. But it was the lack of cultivation and traces of habitation that rendered it 'empty' for Muyu refugees. Initially, the settlement administration had proposed that refugees use land on the northern side of the road, with the southern side reserved for landholders. But refugees had already begun to make gardens and hunt to the south. Gardening land was sought on the edge of rivers and streams inside the East Awin boundary, in preference to the higher inland area which was dry. Observers' accounts support this:

> There was not any plan, and the order in which refugees were relocated became a matter of political expediency which changed from day to day. Similarly, there was not any plan about which groups should be relocated in which place once they reached the relocation site. In the end, this became a matter of refugee choice, influenced above all by access to water and roads.[9]

Choice of garden site at East Awin was determined by water source. People marked their gardens in the forest by felling tall trees and clearing undergrowth. Some erected a sign by sinking a stake vertically into the ground, making a groove or fork into the top of the stake, and then inserting two pickets in a crossed position into the fork. They explained that the installation of signs was not Muyu customary law as their own boundaries had been defined and observed for generations, and were the subject of public knowledge. Muyu borrowed this method of marking from other people at East Awin, and there was no term in the Yonggom language to describe it. Other signs of ownership observed at East Awin included weeding around the base of a food-bearing forest tree such as the *genimo*, inserting pieces of barbed wire or thorns into the trunk of a coconut palm and tying a piece of coarse reed around a tree trunk. These signs indicated several possibilities: ownership in order to discourage theft, death of the tree's owner resulting in the postponement of harvest until after a period of mourning, or simply that the owner wished to rest the tree in order to increase the size of its fruit or harvest. People also entered into spoken agreements with neighbours about mutual boundaries. The act of trespassing violated Muyu custom even at East Awin, and people knew not to enter another person's garden to cut firewood, fish or hunt. Trespassing could anger the other person and lead to a dispute or sanction. People understood that they had rights to the rivers and streams that entered their gardens at East Awin, and to the trees and the animals that lived in the tall grass of that garden.

The notion that a person's cultivated garden at East Awin constituted their own property was only relative. Gardens there were described as a 'garden close by' referring to its proximate and constricted space, and contrasting the owner's prior extensive *dusun*. Some people described their garden at East Awin to be enclosed by the landholder's *dusun*. Land use at East Awin has a generative effect. Using a portion of land by making a garden and planting sago and tree crops, as well as harvesting sago and catching fish beyond the East Awin boundary, can give those 'unnamed' tracts, a human history: 'they ascribe to it a dimension of people's memory'.[10] In another context, Weiner has poetically described how acts such as pausing to inspect fruiting trees, cutting a piece of rattan from a tree overhanging a path, or gathering the edible larvae and leathery nest of a certain moth can turn an unnamed tract into a 'conduit of inscribed activity'.[11]

Markus began cultivating his garden at East Awin in 1987. In his description of it he named some areas with reference to events that had occurred there, and others as descriptive adjuncts:

> There is a place where [people from Atkamba] collect drinking water. The garden near this water source is called the drinking place garden. The area where a tall tree has been felled across the river to make a bridge is called *kimbirimtim* meaning the trunk of a large tree in Yonggom. The area where a banyan tree had previously been felled is known as *irimtim* meaning a tree that has been felled. There is a shallow stream—ankle depth—running through the garden. There is a sago garden. Planted on the edge of the stream are potato, taro, peanuts, bananas, sugar cane, *aibika*, *kumbile*. Previously there was a *kangkung* garden growing on the edge of the stream also. There are breadfruit trees, but the coconut palms

are planted next to my house in the camp—a coconut palm needs the salt from hearth smoke and ash in order to fruit. There is a peanut plot. There is an area of uncleared forest for firewood and building materials. There is a makeshift shelter to sit and rest or get cover from the rain. In the river which flows through the eastern part of the garden, prawns and fish may be caught.

A refugee's garden conceived as bounded personal property is illustrated in two incidents recalled below. The first took place in the market at East Awin where a landholder buyer agreed with a refugee seller to take some fish and return shortly with the money. Some time later, the buyer returned to the seller empty-handed. She explained that she had changed her mind and would not pay money for fish that had been caught outside the East Awin boundary on her own land. Speaking among her friends afterwards, the refugee seller explained that she had caught the fish by her own effort, with a fishing line not poison, from the stream running through her garden located inside the East Awin boundary. She qualified her right to sell the fish based on two points: she perceived the place where she caught the fish, and the effort in catching it, to be hers alone.

The second incident involved rockpool draining, an activity practised by some Muyu who had sufficiently deep streams running through their gardens at East Awin. A group of young men bailed the water from a pool that was located in the garden of a person from a neighbouring camp. The group then collected the prawns and fish from the drained pool. They had not sought permission from the garden owner who claimed that since his wife's death he had intentionally left the pool and surrounding garden idle. His wife had fished and irrigated the garden from this pool prior to her death. The man's claim based on his prior cultivation of the pool and fallow garden was validated, and the young men were each required to pay compensation. Gardens were conceived as private property because of the cultivation efforts of the gardener, and because many refugees claimed that the PNG government had purchased the land of the East Awin settlement in the name of the refugees.

A shelter in one's garden or *dusun* was considered a sign of habitation without which a garden could be considered unoccupied or empty. Some Muyu at East Awin constructed makeshift shelters known as *pondok* in their gardens. A very few were said to have built a *dusun* house in the rainforest outside the East Awin boundary. According to Markus, the landholders ought to receive compensation from the government for any dwellings outside the boundary. In any Muyu *dusun* in the homeland, a shelter or house would be occupied for several weeks at a time during hunting, or sago processing. Muyu people understand their *dusun* house to be their true house. It is a place where they feel at home, for their *dusun* is considered to be their actual place rather than their village house. For older Muyu, composite villages were artefacts of the Catholic Church and Dutch authorities created for the purposes of administration. There is no term in the Yonggom language to describe a village house. Living in a village was simply conceived as living outside one's *dusun*. A village house was a place that one visited. Objects of value and other large items were stored in *dusun* houses rather than village houses, and it was *dusun* houses that were fully equipped.

In contrast, Muyu at East Awin removed their axes, machetes and cooking implements from their *dusun* house or makeshift shelter. This was done because trespassing was rife, boundaries were ambiguous, and people did not always respect each other's property. Some people at East Awin locked their houses with padlocks, others curtained windows with steel mesh. Even locked houses had been broken into. If families were leaving their houses to travel to Kiunga, they would usually invite a neighbour or relative to stay to discourage theft, and to look after chickens or other animals.

During the time I was at East Awin, Samuel—a salaried schoolteacher in his fifties—built a house next to his old house, which was a dilapidated bush hut built on the ground with thatched roof and walls, and no windows. The new house epitomised what refugees described as a 'good' house. It was built 3 metres off the ground, and boasted a tin roof rather than sago thatch, and milled timber walls and flooring rather than adzed bush timber. Samuel's decision to build an elaborate house with full tin roof, guttering, roof trusses, milled timber walls and flooring was commented on by other Muyu. The house was located in a prominent and public position outside the Saint Berthilla Catholic Church, on the edge of the marketplace. Samuel constructed his new house in spite of the offer of permissive residency enabling his family to live elsewhere in PNG, and the other offer of assisted repatriation. But his new house did not reflect his intention to end his journey and remain at East Awin. On the contrary, it reflected his political commitment to remain outside Irian Jaya until *merdeka* had been achieved. By constructing a comfortable house, he was increasing his family's chances of enduring the deprivations of East Awin until it was truly safe to return to the homeland. According to Samuel, the event of *merdeka* was the only truly safe moment to return. Samuel's story illustrates that 'being mid-journey' does not preclude stability or the possibility of a familiar dwelling place.

ENDNOTES

[1] Kumbile (*Dioscorea esculenta*).

[2] Casey, *Getting back into place,* p. 118.

[3] Kirsch, 'The Yonggom of New Guinea', p. 129.

[4] Casey, *Getting back into place,* pp. 114–15.

[5] Casey, *Getting back into place,* pp. 352.

[6] Casey, *Getting back into place,* p. 117.

[7] Debbie Bird-Rose, *Nourishing terrains: Australian Aboriginal views of landscape and wilderness,* Australian Heritage Commission, Canberra, 1996.

[8] I am grateful to Stuart Kirsch for making this connection between emptiness and memory/history.

[9] Preston, p. 864.

[10] James Weiner, *The empty place: poetry, space and being among the Foi of Papua New Guinea,* University of Indiana Press, Bloomington, 1991, p. 41.

[11] Weiner, pp. 38–9.

Chapter 7

Unsated sago appetites

Yakub's house is 2 metres off the ground, its narrow front porch with overhanging sago roof only accessible via a steep ladder. These are not the *kum* steps of Markus's house but a vertical ladder. The slatted floor is made from spindly lengths of black palm. Walking across the floor was a delicate exercise. I initially tried to ensure that my bodyweight was evenly balanced over flattened feet, but quickly learned of the resilient nature of black palm, and the way that it springs back beneath the foot. The sago leaf roof was sooty black, cured by hearth smoke against torrential rain. Yakub's entry room had no furniture. A calendar issued by the local Ok Tedi copper mine was nailed to the wall, and the coloured photographs depicted the livelihoods of Yonggom-speaking people who shared the same language as Muyu, and whose land was contiguous. Several rosary beads were suspended next to the calendar. Curious about a photograph on the calendar, I leaned closer and noticed the word '*duka*', meaning grief or sorrow, written next to a date. I asked Yakub whether the date represented the anniversary of someone's death. Yes, he said, his wife Karolina's mother had died on 25 July because of her yearning for sago.

Yakub related the circumstances of his mother-in-law's death directly to the deprivations of East Awin, particularly the absence of sago. Yakub, with Karolina and her mother, and their children and grandchildren, had travelled into the rainforest on the boundary of the East Awin settlement to cut firewood and harvest their peanut crop. The old woman had returned in daylight so that she could see the path more easily. Insisting on carrying one of her great-grandchildren so that she would not return empty-handed, Karolina's mother had tripped and fallen during the journey home. She had died immediately. Yakub explained: 'She did not want to eat bananas or sweet potatoes, only sago. Every day she would ask if there was any sago. She died from hunger, and yearning for sago.' The old woman's fall and sudden death was explained by Yakub according to a logic of yearning. Muyu from the south ate sago at every meal, they even ate sago by itself. If a Muyu person at East Awin yearned to return to their homeland but could not, their death may be induced by their yearning to eat sago.

The death of Yakub's mother-in-law occurred during the island-wide drought of 1997.[1] The drought profoundly affected refugees at East Awin because there was no naturally occurring sago growing within the camp boundary, and in the event of fire most food plants will burn except sago pith which is insulated by the thick bark of the tree's trunk. A woman in the neighbouring camp composed

'The sago song' to describe the circumstances of Karolina's mother's death. Her paraphrased version follows:

> Thinking of [my] region the sago *dusun*
> With yearning recalling in my heart
> Thinking of the sago gardens in [my] region
> Here there is hunger there is no sago
> Fruits and vegetables are just for the time being
> When the hot season comes then food becomes scarce
> Because of the heat, scorched
> Gradually our strength fades we perish from hunger
> Searching for food entering [the forest] to look for sago
> Anywhere and everywhere in the forest
> Until there are some who fall sick in the forest
> Taken back to the village and die
> Hungry searching for sago travelling far
> Old people have no energy fall sick, die
> In the last dry season we experienced one mother in our village die.

Drought conditions revealed Muyu vulnerability in a place where there was no perennial sago, and the gathering of forest food was restricted. Vegetable plants are not perennial and perish quickly in a dry season. 'The sago song' speaks of states of hunger and survival affected by the absence and presence of sago. During the drought people travelled deep into the rainforest beyond the East Awin boundary, forced to search for sago randomly. Their intimacy with their own *dusun* would never require this. At East Awin however, landowners' proscription of food gathering beyond the camp boundary had rendered the territory foreign. Several times Yakub posed the rhetorical question to me: 'What is the use of being thirsty and hungry in another place in a time of drought?' Although the drought was island-wide, refugees at East Awin recalled their abundant *dusun* exactly as they had left it some 14 years earlier.

During the drought, refugees were forced to virtually abandon their camps in order to follow landholders beyond the East Awin boundary to harvest wild sago. The right to harvest this sago was purchased from the landholders for a price of 50 kina per tree, or 100 kina for a large tree. Individual families purchased trees, and some did so in groups. The Wamena Baptist Church spent 450 kina of church funds to purchase nine sago trees. At Atkamba, a community leader negotiated an arrangement with landholders to allow refugees to fell and mattock sago trees, and then divide the processed sago pith with the tree's owner as compensation. In this way, refugees were able to exchange their labour for sago.

Muyu define themselves using the designation 'sago person'. Many northerners had also relied on sago as a staple food, and although rice competed with sago in coastal towns, adults retained memories of processing sago as children in their parents' village. Sago is a food-starch cultivated from the thick-set trunk of the sago palm which grows to 10 metres in low-lying swamp areas.[2] At maturity, the trunk of the tree becomes engorged with starchy pith which is protected by a 5-centimetre covering of hard bark. After the trunk is felled, the bark is split so that the starch can be extracted, and through a process of kneading, rinsing and straining, the starch forms sediment separated from the woody fibres. This starch can be processed to resemble a kind of flour. A period without sago was conceived as famine or hunger in spite of relative abundance of other crops such as cassava and sweet potato. This is the case for other people and staple foods in the PNG highlands.[3] (In contrast, the Foi of the Hegeso area call their Mubi valley place 'the empty place' or 'the dry place' because there is only sago and no animals for hunting.[4])

In their flight from the homeland, Muyu carried only meagre essentials like sago mattocks. A sago mattock allowed cultivation of a foodstuff that guaranteed their survival. But few Muyu planted sago at East Awin, despite the offer of free seedlings. Planting a sago tree would serve to locate West Papuans at East Awin in PNG. Muyu particularly did not want to imagine themselves still living at East Awin, still living 'outside' their own *dusun* at the time of harvest 10 years on. Muyu resisted cultivating East Awin as a longer-term place of residence. I heard this rationale often: 'On arrival to East Awin we did not plant sago. We wanted independence quickly. We did not want to be here long.'

Markus, who had lived away from his *dusun* since training as a nurse, had planted sago wherever he was. His own experience had taught him to view *dusun* in terms of practice rather than territory: 'Wherever one lives constitutes a *dusun*—wherever one lives or shifts one must plant sago as a sign they are living in that place.' The activity of planting sago expressed Markus's humanity or his Muyuness, regardless of his location. Markus and Yakub, both in their early fifties and employed as health workers at East Awin, had planted sago on their arrival in 1987. Their decision was not simply about consuming the sago pith as flour, it was also about utilising sago palm leaves as roofing material. Their sturdy roofs indicated that they had access to sago palm leaf, but regular cutting of sago leaf for roofing material slowed the production of pith. Such was the importance of roofing material in tropical weather: a dry house was worth at least as much as a sated appetite.

The essential difference between cultivated and wild sago species is that the latter yields less pith, and its leaf is much more porous as thatch. According to Markus, a sago tree's yield may be deduced from signs: the palm leaf's broadrib will be open and bowed toward the ground, and the trunk's girth will be wide. Another test is to chip away a small piece of bark exposing sago pith, then chew the pith and spit onto a leaf. White indicates a high yield. It is commonly understood that an uncultivated tree will produce less flour. A sago palm ought to be harvested before flowering because the flowering process, which occurs after about 12 years, consumes the tree's edible starch. The sight of a sago palm left to flower, its starch wasted, is said to evoke memories of deceased relatives who once prepared sago for the person as a child, or those too old to harvest the flowering palm.[5] The flowering sago palm as a metaphor for barrenness appeared in people's dreams. Where a hunter dreamed of a sago tree that had already flowered it meant that he would snare an old pig with tusks. To dream of a sago tree yet to flower was to catch a young succulent pig.

In the southern Muyu region, the principal sago species used for flour and roofing material grows from shoots that spread from a central plant or are transplanted from elsewhere. This 'cultivated' species cannot be propagated from the seed of fruit that falls to the ground and subsequently consumed by cassowary, or taken by bats and other birds. Cultivated sago is said to mature in three to five years, and has thorns or spikes that must be stripped carefully before the tree is felled. Its leaf is considered the most durable thatching material for roofs, lasting up to six years. By contrast, 'wild' sago refers to naturally growing sago trees that sucker to form extensive groves, or spread via birds and on the water. Wild sago is slow growing and matures after 10 to 12 years. There were no naturally occurring sago stands within the settlement boundary at East Awin, and some people planted local wild sago from suckers gathered by government employees and distributed in 1987. In conversation about the benefits of cultivated versus wild sago, Muyu questioned why inferior sago yielding less flour and porous leaves had been distributed.

This inferior variety also grows in some Muyu regions, but its palm leaf lasts between six months and two years depending on exposure to hearth smoke, and is considered too porous for thatch. While Muyu preferred cooking hearths to be separated from the main living area to avoid smoke inhalation, at East Awin they had been repositioned to the centre of the house for the purposes of curing thatch. It was not even possible to purchase sago palm leaf from Muyu who had planted their own trees at East Awin, because they had sufficient for their own immediate needs only, and were mindful of the pith's harvest. Dani, who were accustomed to thatching roofs from dried grass, experimented with tall, coarse grass. But the grass in the highlands is short, fine and strong—more resilient than the grass at East Awin which decomposes in the wet. Others experimented with the leaves of the (non-fruiting) forest coconut palm and found that it became porous after several months only. Some purchased palm leaf harvested from forest sago, from the landholders. One parcel or *bungkus* comprised seven sheets of palm thatch, and 30 parcels were sufficient to roof a medium-sized house and kitchen. A single parcel cost the equivalent of 1.5 kilograms of rice, or 5 kina.

Refugees expressed sympathy for the landholders' claim for compensation against the settlement. They claimed 1500 kina per landholder family for every year of occupation since 1987. This amount compensated the landholders for loss of tallwood/hardwood trees, cassowaries, pigs and birds. Trees like sago that had been planted by refugees were considered to be a legacy to the landholders, but the question of ownership was ambiguous. Some refugees claimed that landholders had prohibited them from planting sago outside the East Awin boundary, and discouraged planting sago inside the boundary. This response is congruous with a Muyu worldview that special permission is required to plant sago on another person's land, because sago trees perpetually produce suckers that colonise the area of the initial planting, producing an enduring and ambiguous relationship between the planter and the other person's land.[6] To gather wild sago outside the East Awin boundary was also prohibited unless permission from the landholders was sought, and compensation paid. While hunting and fishing was often done without permission, cultivating sago was in a different realm. Markus explained the difference between hunting game or fishing, and gathering sago:

> If you want to look for fish [they] don't gather in the one place. You must make an effort to find and catch fish. A pig, too, roams about, it does not have a particular place. The hunter of the pig takes a risk he may be gored. A sago tree's location is known. It is located in someone's *dusun*. So permission must be granted and payment made.

Markus's point is that the emplaced nature of sago—inside the boundary of certain people's *dusun*—and the deliberation of harvesting, differentiates it from hunting which is entirely reliant on the individual hunter's dexterity.

The sorts of trees which refugees were prohibited from planting included long-living or thick-barked trees: durian, rambutan, mango, citrus, breadfruit, coconut, *ketapang*, pandanus, *soursop* and sago. Muyu stressed that when they returned to their own region, these trees would be left behind for the landholders. But it was said that the descendants of the planter could inherit certain rights to the tree:

> We don't want to take any of this home, we will just leave it here. Although I have planted this sago garden here, if I should return home, they [the landholders] may have it. But if my descendants come here to see what I have left behind, they may have a part [rights of use]. According to the past, whoever planted sago was the owner.

Planting long-living trees and opening new gardens was countered by the knowledge that one's *dusun* lay fecund, wasted. There was a sense of futility about gardening because (imminent) repatriation would render gardening effort at East Awin fruitless. A Biak woman recalled her father's lamentation about such futility. Returning from his garden, exhausted by the effort of clearing tall trees and forest undergrowth, he would sing in Biak in a mournful tone that reduced his granddaughter to frightened tears:

> So weary because I am not working my garden there but here
> How has it happened that I am gardening in another person's land whereas I have a garden there
> How has it happened that I am so weary here making a large garden
> I live in this forest here, only gardening
> I ought to be living on the coast: seeing the beach, going fishing.

The hardship of clearing dense forest, and planting new seedlings that would not bear for several years, contrasted with the memory of their own mature yielding gardens and *dusun*. Ruminating on the abundance of their previous *dusun* caused people to fret about the austerity of their lives at East Awin. Muyu's customary practice of shifting cultivation was severely restricted. Shifting cultivation is sustainable in extensive forest areas with small populations, but not in a place like East Awin where several thousand people were relocated to a restricted area within a few months. Poor soil also hindered Muyu people's cultivation practice. Agronomist surveys of the East Awin site proposed that the area did not have enough land available for shifting cultivation as it was practised in surrounding systems, and that weathering from massive rainfall (about 4 metres annually) had produced acid clay soils with low to moderate capability for tree crops and improved pastures, and low capability for arable crops.[7] While the low fertility of the soil was unable to support more than one agricultural crop, opening new gardens became problematic because of restricted space.

In the gardens at East Awin, at least two crops were planted before they were fallowed to become low woody regrowth. In surrounding areas, there was only one planting before fallowing. Fallow periods of 12 months at East Awin were considerably shorter than the period of 15 years observed in surrounding areas.[8] In their own region and in the border camps, most Muyu had relied on sago for energy. In its absence at East Awin, green banana had become the main carbohydrate staple. Bananas were categorised as a wasteful crop. Banana productivity is high in the first year and declines rapidly compared with peanuts and sweet potatoes planted in rotation, or other vegetables that can be planted in old gardens. Other crops at East Awin included taro, pumpkin, snake beans, cucumbers, *kangkung* (leafy green), *aibika*, lowland *pit pit*, corn, pawpaw, pineapples and up to 20 varieties of banana. From 2003, rice cultivation increased after several mills were installed at East Awin by the Montfort Catholic Church.

Many Muyu at East Awin had previously been dependent on subsistence strategies that required access to uncultivated rainforest tracts: the gathering of uncultivated plants (seasonal fruits, berries, nuts, flower buds and palm hearts), the hunting of edible insects and small animals (grubs, larvae, ants, spiders, grasshoppers, frogs, fish, prawns, lizards and birds), as well as wild pig, cassowary, cuscus, iguana, snakes and bats.[9] While bananas and sago were said to leave people feeling hungry for meat and fat, the rainforest was described as a place of abundance where a person's hunger can be satisfied.[10] At East Awin, game was quickly hunted to the point of extinction and hunting beyond the boundary required permission from the landholders. The extent to which this operated as a normative rule but was not followed in practice is difficult to judge.

Some refugees tried to negotiate rights of use to *dusun* beyond the East Awin boundary. In doing so they were trying to restore practices of everyday life such as sago cultivation and hunting. A group of Muyu purchased 'right of use' to an area of Awin land boasting a sago garden and *ketapang* trees located on the edge of the settlement near the Fly River. The group comprised members of several clans originating from the same or neighbouring villages in Irian Jaya. They had processed sago several times on the land without prior permission before the landholder claimed compensation. Each group member had then contributed pigs and cash sufficient to compensate the owner for past damage, and for ongoing rights of use to the land. The permission was categorised as 'unrestricted' and included the right to lay hunting snares and *tubah* fishing bombs. Subsequently, however, another group of landholders claimed compensation rights to the same area as well as 50 kina for each sago palm felled in the future.

Given the lengths that people went to in order to gain access to sago at East Awin, it is not surprising that women made efforts to simulate the flour. At a performance celebrating the anniversary of the patron saint of the Catholic Church at Yogi camp, some members of the congregation performed a version of the Muyu dance called *ketmom*. The dancing was a procession of vignettes, one of which comprised a man holding a cassava grater made from a flattened milk powder tin punched with nail holes. His sister performed the wringing action necessary to squeeze the sediment from the grated cassava pulp. The father of the brother–sister duo interpreted the cassava vignette: 'It is about wringing cassava. We live at East Awin where cassava has become our staple food, replacing sago.' It is in relation to the other vignettes that 'grating cassava' can be understood as quotidian. These vignettes included: 'combing hair', 'sweeping' and 'planting paddy'.

Photo 3. Grating cassava to become like sago.

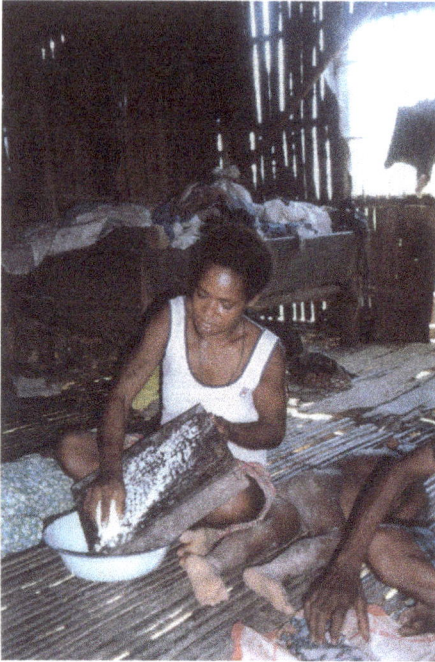

Photo: Diana Glazebrook.

'The cassava song', in the Yonggom language, was performed during the visit of the Diocese's Catholic Bishop to East Awin to officiate in confirmation ceremonies in August 1999:

> Every day I am fed up with eating cassava living at East Awin, hungry, hungry
> We want to return home to the place where we eat sago
> Those of us here want to return soon to our place
> The afternoon bird has called therefore we want to return to our place
> Here is not our place of origin, our place of origin is where the sun goes down.

Consumption of cassava marks Muyu displacement in the song. Perhaps because of its abundance, growing like a weed in everyone's garden at East Awin, people's appetites are unsated by it. In the lyrics, cassava is not mentioned as a food simulated to resemble sago, but it is in the subsequent line 'we want to return home to the place where we eat sago' that the connection between cassava and sago is explicit. The song uses two images popular in Muyu songs of yearning at East Awin: the setting sun and the call of the afternoon bird. Both reference the Muyu region.

Cassava is a perennial woody shrub that has enlarged roots filled with starch.[11] The roots can be boiled and eaten like potatoes, or can be grated, kneaded and rinsed to extract starch which can be processed as a sort of flour. The processing of cassava to imitate sago is contained in the following three expressions: '[cassava] changed to become sago', 'I want to eat the same as there' and 'to resemble the taste of *papeda* because I usually eat this'. Imitation is most obviously contained in 'cassava-sago' which is the term used to refer to grated cassava. At East Awin, people processed cassava to make flour for an unleavened bread which they called baked sago, and to make *papeda*. *Papeda* is a stiff, opaque jelly that is flavoured with meat or fish juices. *Papeda* made from cassava flour was considered to be an inferior imitation of authentic *papeda* made from sago flour. Among Muyu, the fact that sago cannot be simulated may be related to its place in Muyu cultural and social life, as well as its taste and appearance. The activity of sago cultivation involves expedition: journeying together to the tree's site, judiciously selecting a tree, felling the tree, collectively processing pith to become flour (mattocking, rinsing, squeezing), wrapping the flour and carrying it home in procession.

Theory of simulation is revealing in a situation of displacement where absent materials or substances like staple foods become the object of simulation attempts. Baudrillard constructs the categories of simulation and dissimulation, proposing that simulation is not a thing of pretence but something that unsettles the difference between the true and the false, the real and the imaginary. Dissimulation leaves the principle of reality intact, and the difference is always clear.[12] Clearly for Yakub's mother-in-law, and most Muyu people I spoke to at East Awin, cassava cannot simulate sago for the principle of reality is always intact, and the difference is embedded in the name 'cassava-sago'. There are instances of sago simulation elsewhere in New Guinea. For example, East Sepik people who went to West New Britain in the late 1960s and early 1970s as part of an oil palm resettlement scheme, processed the pith of the fishtail palm to imitate sago.[13]

Yakub used the narrative of his mother-in-law's death to foreground his most recent efforts to repatriate residents of his camp at East Awin to their village in the Muyu region. Yakub explained the reason for Muyu flight in 1984, and prolonged exile in PNG, in terms of disenfranchisement produced by the Indonesian state's failed promise of 'development'. Yakub formulated his own development plan and sought co-operation for its implementation from neighbouring regional governments in PNG and Irian Jaya. The plan consisted of four components: a map titled 'Highway Development', a diagram showing the configuration of a new village, an inventory of services necessary to resettle the village, and a human resources inventory of the skills that villagers had acquired since living in PNG. In September 2003, I received an email from Yakub via the Catholic Church in Kiunga:

> Child, my plan has happened, from Mindiptanah to Tubmok. Now the governments of PNG and Indonesia have united to clear the road from Kiunga to Dome [PNG] and on to Tubmok [Irian Jaya]. Father will return home to Tubmok in the year 2004, around February. The reason being: the road is already cleared from Mindiptanah to Tubmok.

Muyu anxiety about returning to the homeland or staying at East Awin manifests a dialectical tension between the virtues of the homeland in spite of neglect and violence, and the possibilities of the host country in spite of landlessness and the absence of sago. It is expressed in the phrase: 'If I stay here there's nothing yet if I return I do not know whether I will be safe.' Yakub's plan partially addressed the bases of fear—identified as isolation and underdevelopment—in returning to the Muyu region. Focusing on infrastructure such as transport, market facility for agricultural produce, schooling, health services, and housing, Yakub has attempted to unsettle this tension by increasing the 'safeness' of the homeland region in relation to the host country.

In 2004, some of Yakub's group returned to the Indonesian Province of Papua. They went to the provincial town closest to their village where they squat in makeshift dwellings on vacant land on the edge of the local airfield. Their neighbours are other Muyu returnees from East Awin who repatriated in 2000 and similarly chose not to return to their villages of origin. Over a 20-year period, some of these original villages built out of bush materials are barely distinguishable from the surrounding rainforest. According to Jacques Gros, it is the absence of schooling in these villages that has drawn Muyu returnees and Yakub's group to the closest provincial town. The road from the international border to Mindiptanah envisaged by Yakub has been constructed. So too, the bridge across the Muyu river. But additional public works at Tubmok have not been undertaken. The impasse is this: Yakub squats in the closest provincial town waiting for evidence of development in order to relocate to his village, and the local government waits for evidence of sufficient population return to justify development of facilities.[14]

Other Muyu returnees have not settled in their *dusun* or village of origin either. In 1986, 34 families were resettled as *translokal* at a transmigration site near Merauke. In 1998, almost half of the families had left the site seeking better opportunities: six families had been assigned to new places as civil servants, some shifted to Merauke town for schooling, while others moved to the neighbouring Muting-Asiki area for economic opportunities.[15] It was reported that neither those families who left the transmigration settlement, nor the ones that stayed, had chosen to return to their *dusun* or village, yet:

They are keenly aware of the fact that they still own traditional land (*dusun*) 'at home'. The rights on this land are watched carefully and normally taken care of by relatives on the spot. If needed they will travel to their land if there is a need to arrange something. They feel quite secure as to their rights and therefore there is hardly any eagerness to move back to their village.

The report implies that Muyu were satisfied with maintaining their *dusun* from a distance. Perhaps it was not that returnees chose to stay away, but that conditions in these abandoned villages (without health clinic, school, transport, market) gave them no option of resettlement there.

What can at least be said of the return of Yakub's camp to the homeland is that even on the edge of the airfield, at a distance of 40 kilometres from his *dusun* and village of Tubmok, he is substantially closer than he was at East Awin.

ENDNOTES

[1] See Bryant J. Allen, 'The 1997–98 Papua New Guinea drought: perceptions of disaster', in R. H. Grove and J. Chappell (eds), *El Nino: history and crisis*, White Horse Press, Cambridge, 2000, pp. 109–22.

[2] Sago (*Metroxylon sagu*).

[3] cf. Ballard, 'The death of a great land: ritual, history and subsistence revolution in the Southern Highlands of Papua New Guinea', PhD thesis, The Australian National University, Canberra, 1995.

[4] Weiner, p. 22.

[5] Kirsch, 'Changing views'.

[6] Schoorl, *Kebudayaan dan Perubahan*, p. 123.

[7] Allen et al., p. 44; P. Bleeker, *Explanatory notes to the land limitation and agricultural land use potential map of Papua New Guinea*. Land Research Series No. 36, Commonwealth Scientific and Industrial Research Organisation, Canberra, 1975, p. 33.

[8] Allen et al., p. 44; Bleeker, p. 79.

[9] Kirsch, 'The Yonggom of New Guinea', p. 201.

[10] Kirsch, 'The Yonggom of New Guinea', p. 201.

[11] Cassava (*Manihot esculenta*).

[12] Baudrillard, *Simulacra and simulation*, p. 3.

[13] Fishtail palm (*Caryota rumphiana*). Mike Bourke, pers. comm.

[14] Jacques Gros, pers. comm.

[15] Jayapura Secretariat of Peace and Justice, 'Situational report on returnees from Papua New Guinea to Irian Jaya dealing in particular with returnees to the Waropko-Mindiptana area', 1998.

Chapter 8

Becoming translokal

After only three years at East Awin, Conrad left in 1995 to make a reconnaissance journey to Irian Jaya to assess the feasibility of permanent return. In his absence, Conrad's *dusun* and that of his neighbours had been levelled to the ground and developed as a transmigration settlement. Local landholders—Conrad's neighbours—had been integrated into the settlement as *translokal*. They had been issued with a 2-hectare land parcel, a prefabricated timber dwelling, and food rations for the first season. Conrad's return to East Awin in 1999 coincided with my research, and over many sessions he recounted the fate of returnees and how they had become local transmigrants known as *translokal*.

By making Conrad's account the material of this chapter I have no pretensions about it being unreservedly subjective, specifically in relation to Kanum relocation and the delineation of Kanum territory. The value of Conrad's account is not as an object for metadiscursive analysis, that is, bringing other research and reports to bear on his version in order to validate it, or mark its deviation from official accounts. Rather, the value is that it stands plainly as a cautionary tale to prospective returnees. Plainly, the action of repatriation risks becoming *translokal*. By foregrounding radical change at the local level, Conrad warns against utopic thinking. Some refugees, despite knowing that the 1997 drought was island-wide, recalled their own *dusun* as fecund and predictable in opposition to drought-ravaged East Awin. Conrad's account reveals how *dusun* have been transformed in people's absence, into partitioned rice paddies populated by Indonesian farmers and retired military personnel.

Conrad's narrative also shifts our focus from the minutiae of settlement at East Awin, to the two journeys on either side: arriving and leaving. It reveals how colonial partitioning of territory, and the intricate histories of groups whose land is contiguous across an international boundary, gets caught up in people's experiences as refugees. Conrad and his Kanum neighbours were classified as refugees and relocated to East Awin because they crossed the international border as citizens of Indonesia. The fact that they claimed land rights in the place where they crossed, and shared language and kin relations with the people there, was finally taken into account on their return in 1995. Muyu refugees were faced with similar dilemmas when they crossed the border as Indonesian citizens and camped on the land of people with whom they shared the Yonggom language and kin relations.

Conrad's account begins with the circumstances of his relocation to East Awin from a border camp. In 1992, following a raid by the Indonesian military on the border town of Sota, 100 families fled on foot for 15 kilometres to a location east of the border near Wereave, a village lying between the towns of Sota to the north west and Weam to the south. After complaints against the Sota group by local landholders, the PNG government and UNHCR arranged for the relocation of the group to East Awin.

To understand the meaning of Kanum crossing boundaries, Conrad classified them based on the locality of their customary land or *dusun*. He differentiated several Kanum clans whose territory lay close to Sota in Irian Jaya. According to Conrad, some Kanum claimed their *dusun* to be around Sota, extending in an easterly direction as far as the Torassi River in PNG. Some claimed their *dusun* to lie to the north, and to the south of Sota. Others claimed their *dusun* lay east of the Torassi River which is inside PNG. From Conrad's point of view, the centre of Kanum-ness, or the point of focus for Kanum, lies around the area that became the township of Sota. Kanum inhabit an area divided by an international boundary. Those who reside to the west are categorised as citizens of Indonesia, and those to the east are citizens of PNG. Kanum in PNG speak a little Indonesian, and Kanum in Irian Jaya speak a little Motu, a PNG lingua franca.

Kanum distinctions became complicated in the 1930s. At that time, Dutch Protestant missionaries established a school and church on Kanum land at a place on the western side of the Torassi River which was named Waia. It was previously a coconut garden, and according to Conrad lay inside Kanum *dusun*. The institutions of church and school drew other Kanum away from their respective *dusun* to the place of Waia. Three years later, the international border was demarcated, and the Australian government claimed that the Dutch school and church were incorrectly located on the eastern side of the border. The Dutch missionaries then relocated their school and church 10 kilometres to the west inside the Netherlands New Guinea boundary, to a place that became known as Sota.

Some Kanum whose *dusun* lay to the west of the Torassi River, followed the mission and relocated to Sota, which was in effect the western most part of their *dusun*. I will call these people Sota Kanum. The *dusun* of Sota Kanum stretched from Sota in the west to the Torassi River in the east. For those Kanum whose *dusun* lay to the east of the Torassi, relocation to Sota would have been too far from their *dusun*. With the school and church at Waia gone, they relocated to the village of Wereave near Waia. These people I will call Wereave Kanum. Those Sota Kanum who vacated the eastern part of their *dusun* when they relocated to Sota, gave rights of use to this *dusun* to other Kanum (i.e., Wereave Kanum). These rights to land given to Wereave Kanum were merely 'rights of use', as it was considered that they sustained full rights to their own *dusun* further to the east. Conrad defines rights of use (as opposed to rights of ownership) as provisional: 'those with rights of use must surrender this right if it is reclaimed by the *dusun* owner. Rights of use cannot be practised forever. There will come a time when these rights are withdrawn by the the *dusun* owner.'

In 1992 after the Indonesian military raid, residents of Sota who were both Indonesian citizens and Kanum sought refuge aross the international border in PNG. They were eventually housed in UNHCR tents, and they gathered food from the surrounding *dusun* as though they had rights to that land. They formed a makeshift settlement on an area of land that lay between the international border and the western bank of the Torassi River in PNG. According to Conrad, this was the land that Sota Kanum had vacated in the 1930s, and for which rights of use had been subsequently granted to Wereave Kanum. With this history in mind, some Sota Kanum reasserted their right of ownership. Wereave Kanum protested that the land in question lay inside PNG and that Sota Kanum were Indonesian citizens. Wereave Kanum argued that Sota Kanum were border crossers, and Sota Kanum argued that they were the original inhabitants. The Wereave Kanum who had been settled since the 1930s on *dusun* around Wereave became increasingly anxious. Finally they made a formal complaint to the government, claiming Sota Kanum to be Indonesian citizens who had resettled themselves in PNG on land that was not their own. Conrad, himself a Sota Kanum, defended the claim that Sota Kanum *dusun* extended across the international border as far as the Torassi River in PNG. In the process of the PNG Government and UNHCR handling the dispute, all the people of Sota camped near Wereave were classified as refugees, and were relocated to East Awin. Conrad said: 'According to customary law, we [Sota Kanum] had full rights to resettle at Wereave and resume our *dusun* activities of hunting, harvesting sago and gardening. But according to the PNG government, we were foreigners—refugees.'

Wereave Kanum used their national citizenship to trump ethnicity. Conrad viewed it as expedient: 'Kanum people don't consider there is an international boundary between the (border) towns of Sota and Weam. Whereas others [Indonesian tourists] once they go past the border marker which is decorated with state symbols including Pancasila, they consider themselves in a foreign country outside of their own country.' Conrad said that before the international boundary was marked by a post, the area was *polos* meaning 'blank'. 'Blank' in this context means contigious, continuous, undifferentiated. Aside from the border post, a monument known as Sabang Merauke was installed at the entry point to Sota township in 1987. The monument's title invokes the trope of the Indonesian archipelago: from Sabang (in the west i.e., Sumatra) to Merauke (in the east i.e., Irian Jaya). The garuda eagle, official seal of the Indonesian state, perches above it. The monument symbolically delineates the boundaries of the archipelago. For those living on its margins, like West Papuans, the trope draws their identity westward and back towards the centre, away from the margins and 'Melanesia' to the east.

The movement of Kanum is regulated to some extent by the border, and they must carry identification. Those from the west cross to the east for hunting and gardening because land in the west has become barren, and game is still abundant in the east. People from the east crossing to the west must carry the yellow pass issued by the PNG government, and people from the west crossing to the east must carry the red pass of the Indonesian government. These passes permit the holder to live for six months in the other place, and allow freedom of movement within the Kanum region. As Conrad said:

> Before 1992 we had to approach the Neighborhood Association and request permission to obtain a border pass with the reason for example, 'I want to fetch fish from the Torassi river and visit my relatives there.' An official letter would be issued stating that 'this person has been given permission'. This letter then had to be taken to the Village Secretary to make a travel pass that would then be signed and stamped by the Village Head. But since the change, since Suharto fell, the border pass system has changed. Now I must take my residence identification card with a passport photo to the Immigration Office. A stamped red border pass will be issued. We just arrive and request: 'I want to go there [Weam]' and can request a pass for up to six months.

Some Kanum land on both sides of the border has been classified by the respective states as conservation areas. To the west, Sota is part of the Wasur National Park of Indonesia, and to the east, Weam is a part of the Tonda Wildlife Management Area of PNG. Wasur regulations prohibit Kanum people from hunting native species such as cassowary, pig and kangaroo—only deer may be hunted. But Kanum are allowed rights to firewood collection using traditional tools such as axes, and hunting rights with bows and arrows. On the Indonesian side, Kanum have been registered and photographed. Identification as Kanum permits access to their customary land for the purposes of hunting game.

Conrad remembered Sota as a well-serviced place. Most houses were connected to mains water and electricity. Streets were lit, houses were lit, and even outhouses or toilets had lights. Roofs were made of tin, and people had fences with front gates. In comparison, Wereave across the border was a rural village: houses had thatch roofs, and had neither running water nor electricity. East Awin resembled Wereave, except that they had to build their own houses and thatch their own roofs. At East Awin, the Sota group named their camp 'Weski' after the villages they had reached at the end of their flight path. 'Weski' referenced the PNG villages of Weam and Suki. During the initial five months, Weski refugees received tinned fish and rice rations. But people complained that they had not been issued with roofing material like other refugees who had been issued with a 'one off' supply of reinforced plastic. Weski refugees were forced to make thatch from the porous leaves of forest coconut palm.

According to Conrad, before being airlifted to East Awin, Sota people received a letter from the Indonesian government. The letter warned that their *dusun* would be developed as a transmigration settlement if they did not return. Later, at East Awin they received a second letter from the government inviting them to return to help develop the new transmigration settlement. Ninety-four families decided to return to Irian Jaya in 1993. Some had not even moved out of the temporary UNHCR shelters in which they had been housed since their arrival 12 months earlier. Conrad explained that the Sota group from Weski camp chose repatriation for several reasons: they felt intimidated and disillusioned by the political dynamic at East Awin where factions recruited each other's supporters; they were reluctant to build new houses when they had left far more comfortable ones behind; and with suspension of rations they felt they would be unable to subsist from a small garden alone. Additionally, they perceived East Awin to belong to antagonistic landholders who had not been adequately compensated. According to Conrad, repatriation was not a difficult decision to make, for at the time of departure the deprivations of East Awin seemed to outweigh the risks of return. He used an aphorism to explain the decision as black and white: 'those returning home live, those remaining die'.

Under the auspices of the UNHCR, 94 families were repatriated to Irian Jaya. They were not relocated to Sota however. Instead, the Indonesian government housed them in an empty section of an existing transmigration site on the outskirts of the southern city of Merauke. According to Conrad, they lived in Merauke for 12 months and were 're-educated' in the principles of the Indonesian state philosophy of Pancasila. Pancasila comprises principles regarded as the ideological foundation of the Indonesian nation-state including belief in God, the sovereignty of the people and national unity. An investigation was undertaken into the incident of their flight into PNG, and some refugees were interrogated. From Merauke they were eventually relocated back to 'Sota' but the township as they remembered it no longer existed. Their ancestral land had been purged: cleared and levelled. Three coconut plantations had been cleared as well as bamboo stands, and mango, orange and rose fruit trees. *Dusun* houses indicating ownership and occupation had been demolished. According to Conrad, after fleeing Sota in 1992, the *dusun* surrounding it was annexed by the government. The absent landholders were considered to be political fugitives—law breakers—by virtue of their action of flight across the international border. The village head was then forced to sign over the land without agreement from the actual landholders who had been relocated to East Awin. According to Conrad, seizing Kanum land in their absence was expedient and it followed a logic of retaliation.

A church was all that remained of the former town of Sota, known as 'Old Sota'. Conrad mapped the town, using coloured pencils to delineate the sections of the transmigration settlement. The main street or Sota Road partitions two areas of the transmigration settlement known as Sota I. These two areas contain over 300 families. Each area consists of two parallel rows, four in total. The parallel rows are divided again into sections, and each row consists of six sections. Sota I resembles a suburban subdivision of land, only each section contains several segregated plots and houses. The population is also purposefully configured. Sota Kanum returnees from East Awin live in the northern section, alongside other West Papuans who are not local and retired military personnel known as *transpensiun*. The latter receive a government pension, a standard prefabricated house, and rations, in return for surveillance activity. Transmigrants from Java are accommodated in the southern section of Sota I. All settlers are issued with prefabricated housing made of softwood timber. Flooring is dirt, and those settlers who prefer a concrete floor must pay for it themselves. For Kanum, living on a dirt floor signifies their displacement. They prefer to build their houses off the ground on stilts, because they believe that breeze should flow through a house and that ground-level houses are negatively affected by steam that rises from the earth.

At Old Sota, some coconut palms, banana palms and orange trees remained. Sago stands were also preserved intact because they were on lower ground in a valley. Although Kanum are resident in Sota I as *translokal*, they pick fruit, cultivate the land of Old Sota for gardening and gather pandanus leaves from nearby swamps to make mats and bags. They also use their passes to access their *dusun* to the east of the border around the Torassi River.

Appadurai's theorising of neighbourhood illuminates transmigration settlements as a social formation.[1] It is the subversive potential of neighbourhoods that causes the state to police them like they do borders. Indonesian transmigration settlements are spatially and socially partitioned, and surveillance is embedded. This formation or configuration effectively 'localises' transmigrants and *translokal*. Here 'localise' refers to being corralled, surveyed and managed. Conceivably, West Papuan *translokal* and Indonesian transmigrants continue to seek to produce and reproduce their own neighbourhoods and localities within the transmigration settlement. Their efforts might be undermined by the activities of military personnel who seek to deter the production of locality among residents. Yet the administration is not totalising and may even unintentionally create an environment that supports locality, for example, by permitting Kanum *translokal* to undertake hunting and cultivation activities in their own *dusun* outside the transmigration settlement.

Devastation of ancestral *dusun* at Sota meant the eviction of landholders' ancestral spirit beings that connect Kanum as descendants to their ancestors. Conrad believed that emplaced ancestral spirits would have fled in terror once the felling and clearing began. These spirits known as *dema* [2] to Kanum speakers, are deceased ancestors who may take the form of a particular animal and dwell in natural landscape features. Evicted from their dwelling places, *dema* seek out places similar to those destroyed: a banyan tree or another very large old tree, a sago or bamboo stand, or a large rock formation. A landholder may cultivate a flower garden, or plant a betelnut tree, kava (*wati*) plant or sago tree to entice the wandering *dema* to settle. If a *dema* has not settled in another dwelling place, it will wander and become a risk to local people, especially small children. Settled *dema* offer protection and prosperity to living descendants, who must offer alms such as betelnut or cooked food in return. A *dema* may detach itself from a descendant if they neglect to offer alms, in which case a descendant's wellbeing can be negatively affected.

The disappearance of *dema* makes its descendants vulnerable: 'If its place is damaged, disturbed, it will flee to a new place. The original place will become barren, and the inhabitants of that place will no longer be looked after.' During the process of clearing Sota, a bulldozer operator felling a tree was crushed to death when the tree fell on him. Conrad interpreted the incident in terms of *dema* retaliation: the felled tree had been the dwelling place of a *dema*. If the Indonesian government had compensated the Kanum landholders, the latter could have reassured the *dema* and no recourse would have been required. Conrad would excuse neither Javanese transmigrants nor the Indonesian authorities for ignoring the rights of landholders and their ancestral spirits. For throughout the archipelago and including Java, people believe in their own ancestral spirits in their own place and offer alms routinely.

An evicted *dema* surprised in daylight may assume a human form such as a small child. It had happened that:

> A *dema* which inhabited a place which was built into a soccer field became crowded out and fled into the forest because its place was destroyed. An Indonesian soldier saw it sitting beneath a tree in the forest crying and shot the *dema* thinking it was OPM. The *dema* fled deeper into the forest but returned that night to slash the soldier with a machete. It was only the intervention of an old person from Sota who spoke with the *dema* that saved the soldier's life (Conrad).

In Conrad's story, the identity of the ancestral spirit or *dema,* and the OPM freedom fighter, is merged. The Indonesian soldier mistakes the *dema*, whose identity is bound to territory, for an OPM fighter, whose struggle is against the alienation of Papuan land. Both *dema* and OPM fighter weep over the occupation of their place, and their marginalisation. The Indonesian soldier, completely oblivious to the vulnerability of the weeping figure, is trained to shoot on sight. The soldier seeks to eliminate the person that he suspects as OPM. But ancestral spirits are not mortal, and their defence of their descendants and 'possession' of their ancestral land cannot be extinguished. They have an enduring metaphysical connection with a geographical territory. When the wrath of the displaced ancestral spirit is pitted against the Indonesian soldier in an action of retaliation, it is the mortal descendant of the ancestral spirit, an old person from Sota, who intervenes to save the life of the soldier. As descendant, the old person is part of the same metaphorical field as the *dema*. His compassionate intervention to save the soldier's life invokes the humanity of OPM fighters usually represented as less than human.

The projection that Indonesian soldiers view all Sota people as OPM sympathisers acted as a deterrent to some Weski returnees. Many chose not to return to Irian Jaya. Instead, they made use of their rights to Kanum *dusun* lying between the international border and the Torassi River in PNG. Relocation to Wereave was not straightforward however. After their return from East Awin to Wereave in 1995, negotiations with PNG government officials resulted in Wereave being partitioned in two. 'New Wereave' was relocated 4 kilometres to the east of the original village of Wereave, which was subsquently designated 'Old Wereave'. Those Wereave Kanum who had been resident since the 1930s were relocated to New Wereave, and lost rights to the hunting ground and sago and cocount stands around Old Wereave. Sota Kanum returnees settled at Old Wereave on the Torassi River, and registered as citizens of PNG. Wereave Kanum call them 'refugees', identifying them as stateless people living outside their actual *dusun*.

Forced migration can simultaneously render refugees vulnerable to violence, and in the process of resettlement refugees may have no real choice but to engage in actions that violate the land of others. Conrad's elaboration about loss of *dusun* and displaced *dema* offer insight into the way Kanum and others experienced living as refugees at East Awin. In conversation with Conrad and Muyu interlocutors, I recorded use of the Indonesian term '*keramat*' meaning 'sacred and possessing supernatural qualities', to refer to sites like churches and ancestral land. I also recorded use of the Indonesian infinitive '*rusak*', meaning 'to damage' or 'to spoil', when referring to destruction wreaked on a site considered to be sacred. Many refugees projected that the Awin landholders of the UNHCR settlement site viewed the refugee population to be spoiling their ancestral land. Of the refugee population, it was Kanum and Muyu—who sustained deep attachment to their own *dusun*—who tended to project themselves as spoiling the sacred character of Awin land.

It is not coincidental that Kanum and Muyu are practising Catholics, and also sustain concurrent beliefs in a metaphysical realm, ascribing agency to other non-human inhabitants of the landscape. The approach of the Montfort Catholic Church of the Diocese of Daru-Kiunga which includes East Awin, is syncretic. By this I mean that concurrent beliefs in custom and the gospel are accepted.

For example, former East Awin resident priest Jacques Gros explained Christianity to me as a 'meta-cosmic' belief system that does not abolish 'cosmic' systems which are ancestral, but merely covers them, or lands on them like a hover plane. Kanum and Muyu projections about spoiling Awin sacred land are entirely congruous with a conception of ancestral land as enspirited. From a Muyu worldview, every place is a *dusun* possessed by the spirits of deceased landowners buried there. Making a garden on someone else's land without the permission of the landowner, and the spirits of his ancestors, is to deny the *keramat* character of these places. These ancestral spirits protect the interests of their descendants in that place, and non-descendant dwellers may be considered foreigners unless acknowledgment or compensation is arranged. It was the fact that Conrad and the others were not descendant from ancestral spirits capable of acting malevolently to people identified as foreigners, that was the source of their vulnerability at East Awin.

Among Muyu and Kanum refugees particularly, the sentiment of being an agent of 'desecration' at East Awin has not been conducive to a process of settling. It is one factor among several (including the absence of the staple food sago, famine during the 1997 drought, general food insecurity and antagonistic landholders) that has tended to inhibit settling. The dual sense of 'being desecrating' and being displaced sustains their yearning to return to their own *dusun* where they might resume relations with their own ancestral spirits and restore their autonomy as landowners over a familiar and secure place. At East Awin it was Kanum and Muyu who expressed feelings of weakness and loss. Whereas urban northerners tended to express their hardship at East Awin in terms of material deprivation, and more abstract concepts like discrimination and lack of rights.

The real prospect of becoming *translokal* acts as a deterrent to repatriation, particularly among Muyu whose region now supports vast transmigration settlements constructed since 1984. Even a formally negotiated repatriation program cannot protect returnees from being reintegrated as *translokal*. In the mid-1990s, Yakub joined an observation party comprising three other refugees from East Awin, a Red Cross representative from Jakarta and the East Awin camp administrator. The group was escorted to Merauke to observe the conditions of returnees, and to meet with local government officials, and military officials. Yakub recalled:

> We asked [them]: 'Is it true or not that people who return are tortured with electric current?' The government official answered: 'Yes, there is no problem to both questions.' Then we travelled under escort to transmigration sites and spoke with refugees who had been resettled. They could not speak freely but we gathered their long-term safety was not certain. [I ask:] 'Are they being treated well to entice other refugees to return? Is it a trap? Will we all be punished later, after our return?'

According to Yakub, one of the motivations of the Indonesian government in hosting the visit was to showcase regional development. This is not surprising as the Indonesian government claimed that it was uneven development that had enticed Muyu people to cross into PNG as economic refugees. The visiting party was shown a straight road surfaced with ashphalt that connected Merauke to other parts of the region. Yakub was not unimpressed by such an engineering feat: 'you can see approaching vehicles as a speck in the distance'. But Yakub remained unconvinced that the life of a *translokal* was a sustainable one. Being *translokal* would realise their worst fears at the time of fleeing in 1984: that their ancestral land would be appropriated, and they would become objects of the state.

ENDNOTES

[1] Appadurai, pp. 182–8.

[2] J. Van Baal, *Dema, description and analysis of Marind Anim culture (South New Guinea)*, Martinus Nijhoff, The Hague, 1966.

Chapter 9

Permissive residents

It was not the fact that six of her seven children had just been diagnosed with tuberculosis that Gisela had not slept the night before our visit. It was because of the torrential rain. Her roof comprised scraps of iron and bark, and thick plastic that had been ripped and torn by the winds. In a storm the plastic funnelled the water into the house. She had no money to purchase sago thatch, and no energy to harvest the leaves of the forest coconut palm. On stormy nights, resourceful Gisela would send her children, aged between five and sixteen, to the dry houses of neighbours. It was not just Gisela who weathered these storms. Everyone talked about their roofs at East Awin. Without decent roofing material, people spent rainy nights moving objects away from puddles and rescuing foodstuff and clothing from persistent drips. Torrential rain and fierce winds brought dampness and people complained of aching bones, but the inevitable hot morning sun baked the clay loam all over again.

Like most people at East Awin, Gisela yearned to return to her own village near Sota in Irian Jaya. (It was Gisela's husband who accompanied Conrad back to Irian Jaya in his reconnaisance journey mentioned previously.) But it was the matter of bride-price that made return unsafe for Gisela and her children. On the day after the storm, I invited the UNHCR field officer to accompany me to her house. An economist from Japan, he was busy gathering data for a UNHCR inventory and consulting with refugee leaders. He made several trips to East Awin from the UNHCR Regional Office in Canberra during the time of my research, and was seen wandering in and out of machinery sheds, clipboard in hand, and curious observers in tow. He had no Indonesian or pidgin facility himself, so Hiro talked mainly to refugees who spoke English. As it was only teachers and their students who spoke English at East Awin, the refugee houses that Hiro frequented were teachers' houses. There he might have found cloth curtains covering windows and suspended over doorways, a hand-embroidered tablecloth, a chair to sit on, a kerosene lantern lit at dusk and a battery-powered radio at news time. He would have been offered drinking water in a glass, a cup of sweet black tea and fried banana or some other sweet morsel on a plate.

Gisela's house consisted of two rooms separated by a door. A kitchen had once been attached to the back of the house but had become separated from the main building. Its posts swung beneath the floor and its plastic roofing flapped in the wind. With the kitchen fallen off, Gisela had relocated the cooking hearth to the centre of the main room. She had built it onto a small sheet of corrugated iron, delineated by four sturdy poles of banana palm resembling green bamboo.

On the day of our visit Gisela was absent. She had gone fishing for small fish—the size of a large sardine and filled with bones—in the shallow streams that flowed on the margins of the East Awin settlement. I was told by a neighbour that Gisela never caught much but she adored fishing. Her boys were not idle either and spent their days slingshotting birds and lizards for food. None of her children had attended school at East Awin beyond the second grade. At different times, Gisela had temporarily adopted her older children out to other families in neighbouring camps. On the morning of our visit, the younger children were sitting around the hearth, which was smoking because of damp wood. They were boiling cassava in the household's only cooking pot, a large aluminium saucepan with a hairline crack that emitted steam. There was no crockery, no cutlery. At East Awin, Gisela was reliant on the generosity of her neighbours, of whom three earned wages. The family survived on cassava and small fish, and contributions such as salt and occasionally rice, as well as soap and old clothes.

It was Gisela's neighbour who told me a version of Gisela's life story. Gisela's own place was replete with deer and pig meat, sago and coconut. She had never experienced hunger before arriving to East Awin. A raid was carried out by the Indonesian military on her border village in 1992, on the pretext that villagers were suspected of harbouring OPM fugitives. Much of the population fled to the east across the international border into PNG. They camped near Weam in Moorehead Province for several months before being officially relocated to East Awin. Gisela and her husband and five children were relocated with another one hundred families. At East Awin, Gisela gave birth to two more children. Three years after their arrival at East Awin, Gisela's husband travelled with Conrad, by foot and canoe, back to their border village to see what had taken place. From East Awin, Gisela heard the news that, following custom, her husband had married his older brother's widow. Some time later, a neighbour at East Awin heard of Gisela's husband's death on the local radio's 'deceased listing', broadcast nightly from the capital Jayapura.

Gisela's travesty was that her husband had never submitted bride-price to her family. Among Yei and Kanum, bride-price customarily meant the exchange of sisters and Gisela's husband had not submitted a sister or female relative to Gisela's family.[1] Ignoring exchange brings grievance and retribution. Gisela's husband's sudden and inexplicable death rendered Gisela's family vulnerable to accusation of sorcery. For according to the logic of retribution, Gisela's family was the most aggrieved party. Gisela and her children were barely surviving at East Awin, but the act of return posed different threats. If she returned to her husband's family they might seek to avenge their son's death which they believed was caused by Gisela's family. Returning to Gisela's own family would increase their vulnerability. Even at a distance of several hundred kilometres from her village, Gisela felt the threat of retribution of her husband's family. This was evidenced by the recent diagnosis of six of her seven children with tuberculosis, and Gisela's own blinding headaches, sleeplessness and inexplicable bodily sensations. She felt like someone was following her and could sense their breath on the nape of her neck. The neighbour who told me Gisela's story did not understand why Gisela's husband had not submitted a sister from his side of the family in exchange. Ignoring the rules of exchange risks antagonistic feelings between both parties, and bad feelings inspire retribution through such means as sorcery. In contrast, exchange cements relations between families by equalising loss and gain.

The matter of bride-price profoundly shaped Gisela's decision whether to return to the homeland, or remain at East Awin. The decision of returning or staying cannot be reduced entirely to macro politics. For some people categorised as refugees, decision-making may be bound up in cultural matters. Gisela's story although anomalous, allows us to see displacement from the margins. Experiences like hers might be conceived as the 'trash of history'[2] for her circumstances do not fit the archetypal West Papuan refugee, whose flight into exile in order to struggle for freedom will be followed by eventual return. In historian Neumann's writing, inspired by Benjamin, he looks for a past that seems useless, in the sense that it cannot be used to delineate the present: 'These fissures, breaking up the continuity that is constructed between past and present ... enable us to glimpse the otherness of the past and the potential otherness of the future.'[3] There is no political sense in Gisela's existence at East Awin. She and her children are only incidentally there. She fled east across the international border to save her and her children's lives, and to follow her husband who may or may not have harboured OPM. By relocating his family to East Awin, Gisela's husband was merely falling in step with the decision of the main group. Staying on at East Awin allows Gisela to (mostly) avoid the imbroglio of suspicion and accusation that would be her fate if she returned. Her vulnerability—her unpaid bride-price—was exposed by the events that had removed husband and wife from their respective families and from each other.

Gisela was not the only person at East Awin troubled by the changes to PNG refugee policy that offered the 'choice' of joining an assisted repatriation program to Irian Jaya, or registering for permissive residency and remaining in PNG. For Gisela, the so-called choices would effect similar ends. Returning would surely result in her death by sorcery and staying could see her children die from poverty-induced disease. During a meeting in a church at East Awin in 1997, a government official briefed the congregation on the subject of the new policy. Markus recounted the incident to me. During the course of the meeting, a congregation member expressed his dilemma to the official: 'If I stay here there is nothing, yet if I return, I don't know whether I will be safe.' The man, who was moved to rise from his seat, articulated eloquently the dilemma of decision-making for people unable to find solace in a decision to return to the homeland, or remain in the host country. For in the homeland they have 'everything' yet they are unsafe, and in the host country they are safe yet they have 'nothing'. Like Gisela, the man saw both options carrying considerable risk.

Ironically, refugees and their advocates had lobbied for the status of 'permissive resident' since the mid-1980s. It was not until the offer was made, and the terms and conditions explained, that people understood the effects of the status change and began to question its benefit. To understand permissive residency it is necessary to trace a prior shift in status, from border crosser to refugee. Use of the term 'permissive residency' dates back to the 1960s. At this time, the Australian administration of PNG issued temporary entry or permissive residency permits on humanitarian grounds to West Papuans crossing the border. These permits required holders to refrain from political activity relating to Irian Jaya and could be revoked by the Administrator.[4]

Other people moving west–east across the border were classified as 'traditional border crossers'. Their movement was considered temporary in character for the purposes of traditional activities listed as: 'social contacts and ceremonies including marriage, gardening, hunting, collecting and other land usage, fishing and other usage of waters, and customary border trade.'[5] The Migration Ordinance of 1963 contained no clear provisions for dealing with non-traditional border crossers and assessment of their status was at the colonial Administrator's discretion.[6] By determining asylum applications individually, the Australian, and later, PNG administrations, in effect masked the political nature of the movement.[7] Generally speaking, the PNG government preferred to categorise West Papuans as border crossers rather than refugees. This avoided predetermining their status, and encouraged repatriation as the most appropriate response.[8] It was not until the influx of 11,000 West Papuans between 1984–86 that the question of status became a sensitive topic for the national Cabinet and press. It was argued that those who had crossed en masse could not be categorised according to the technical term border crosser, as their movement was not temporary in character or for the purpose of traditional activities.

A discourse of 'Melanesian-ness' was invoked in the press and Cabinet, naturalising PNG solidarity with West Papuans. An English-language play titled 'My brother my enemy' by PNG writer John Kasaipwalova, written in 1978, explores fraternity when it pushes up against nation-state politics. The relations of diplomacy between nation-states, rather than the relations of kin or shared Melanesian-ness, shape political decisions. The play traces the response of the PNG Security Minister (Sokaru) to the arrest of his cousin Sari, an OPM leader. Sokaru, a Minister in the Cabinet, never pauses to reflect on his cousin's struggle in light of his own post-colonial state. The two were raised as brothers in a village in the border province of Sandaun. Sari's identity was determined by two events: his father's decision to relocate from the border town of Vanimo to his wife's village in the highlands and the annexation of Netherlands New Guinea by Indonesia. Sari's legal status as a citizen of Indonesia renders his re-entry without a visa into PNG to be illegal. His political activity is also deemed criminal by both PNG and Indonesia. Sokaru's uncles invoke their kinship relation to Sari by bringing a pig, and foodstuff, to Sari in jail. It is via their uncles' actions that Sokaru's identity as Sari's cousin becomes known. Sokaru the politician undercuts the fraternal values of the 'Melanesian way': not only does he treat his cousin Sari as an enemy, he joins hands with his own cousin's enemy (Indonesia).

Photo 4. 'Who's [sic] put the border mark!' Oil painting by Herry Offide, 1999.

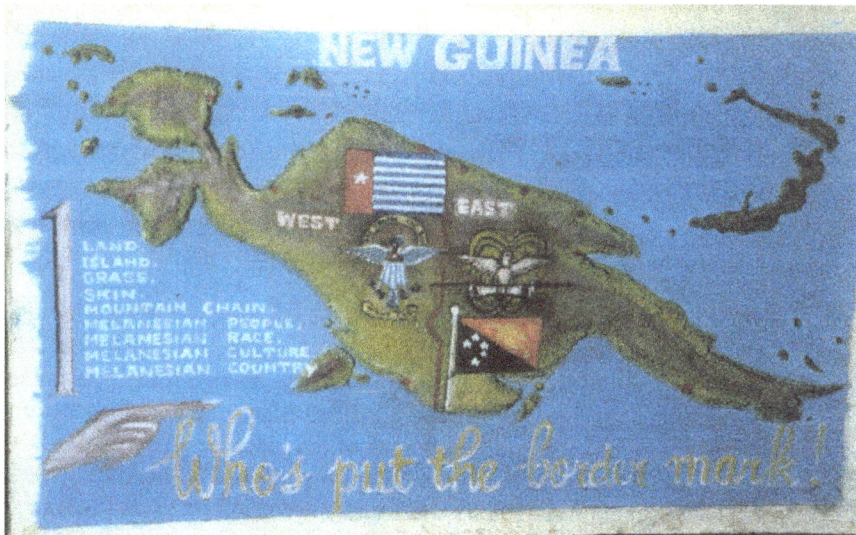

Photo: Diana Glazebrook.

Among PNG policy-makers in the 1980s, it was the economic refugee argument that came to dominate thinking on the matter of asylum.[9] PNG did not challenge Indonesia's claim that border crossers were motivated by non-political or economic motives. Indonesia promoted a theory of underdevelopment that claimed cross-border movement to be the result of unequal development in the border region.[10] Simply, West Papuans were pulled across the border by opportunities on the PNG side. While deliberations continued about the status of the West Papuans as border crossers or political refugees, there were threats of repatriation and incidents of deportation. Some people also returned of their own accord. Between 1984 and 1988, as many as 2150 West Papuans were reported as voluntarily returning to Irian Jaya. Among them was a group of about 140 who were 'repatriated' without UNHCR monitoring, and about 12 who were recorded as deported.[11]

PNG's public support of Indonesia's sovereignty over Irian Jaya can be traced back to the pre-1975 period when PNG acted as understudy to Australia in the negotiation of a Border Agreement with Indonesia. PNG's continued economic relationship with Australia influenced the former's foreign policy. Analysts have said that PNG's perception of its own vulnerability in relation to Indonesia compelled the government to 'accept the Indonesian interpretation of the Border Agreement and to implement it accordingly, or at least, to appear to implement it.'[12]

While the national Cabinet and press bickered about the status of West Papuans who had crossed en masse in 1984, the Australian Section of the International Commission of Jurists (ICJ) advised that: 'the approximately 11,000 border crossers ... were either refugees under the UN Convention and Protocol, or were clearly in a refugee-like situation within the mandate of the UNHCR'.[13] Based on their mass influx, UNHCR recognised them as prima facie refugees. However, it was not until a famine caused the death of 51 West Papuans at Komokpin border camp between July and August 1984, that the PNG relented and accepted UNHCR intervention. It was estimated that over 2000 refugees were squatting in an area at Komokpin that ordinarily provided for only 150 people.[14] The PNG Cabinet agreed to accede to the Geneva Convention and protocol relating to the status of refugees in January 1986, and the Convention entered into force in October.[15] The PNG government and the UNHCR signed an agreement which provided UNHCR funds to resettle West Papuans in PNG until the end of 1986. The UNHCR was given responsibility for administering the border camps in consultation with the PNG Department of Provincial Affairs and in consultation with Indonesia.[16]

Under the 1978 PNG Migration Act, permissive residency status could be accorded to refugees for renewable periods of three years, conditional on no political activity and residence outside the border area.[17] An international campaign lobbied the PNG government to offer permissive residency to West Papuan refugees. In spite of PNG's ratification of the UN Convention, which prohibited refoulement or forced return to Irian Jaya, lobbyists argued that permissive residency status would remove any risk of refoulement. Permissive residency would also mitigate the impact of the government's reservations to Article (26) of the 1951 Convention, by permitting freedom of movement within PNG. It was not until 1996 that the government announced the change in policy, and not until the following year that application procedures for permissive residency were finalised.

Several conditions were attached to the offer of permissive residency status: 1. To abide by the laws of PNG; 2. Not to engage directly or indirectly in any political activity that might affect the good relationship between the governments of PNG and Indonesia; 3. Not to reside in the border areas of West Sepik and

Western Provinces except East Awin camp; 4. Not to engage directly or indirectly in OPM activities including holding of military and civil positions in the organisation; 5. Not to hold executive positions nor be financial members of any political parties in PNG; 6. Not to vote or stand in national, provincial and local government elections in PNG until attainment of citizenship; 7. To notify the appropriate authority of any change of address and place of residence in PNG; and 8. Permits are subject to renewal annually.

Permissive residents would have the following rights: 1. Free movement within PNG except to and in border areas; 2. Engagement in business activities including leasing of government land and access to banking facilities; 3. Employment with similar conditions as nationals; 4. Enrolment in PNG schools and tertiary institutions; 5. Access to health services and facilities; 6. Access to PNG courts; 7. Freedom of worship; 8. Freedom of marriage; 9. Eligibility for naturalisation after eight years qualifying period as permissive residents; and 10. Freedom to return to Indonesia again to take up permanent residency at own expense.

According to Indonesian law (Article 17(k) of the Indonesian Basic Law No 62 of 1958), West Papuans at East Awin have lost their Indonesian citizenship, as their absence from Indonesia has exceeded five years.[18] Under Section 67 of the PNG Constitution, permissive residents are eligible for PNG citizenship after eight years. Refugees interpreted the meaning of citizenship differently. Some claimed that citizenship was only something written on paper, and a bureaucratic necessity that did not alter their sense of themselves as 'Muyu' or 'Dani', or West Papuans. Others felt that becoming PNG citizens would diminish their struggle to restore their West Papuan nationhood. It is probable that the children of West Papuan refugees who have been born and raised in PNG—some 52 per cent of the population at East Awin—may view the prospect of citizenship differently. In 2004, UNHCR issued birth certificates to all children under the age of twenty born in PNG. A birth certificate provides a legal identity which is not a document of citizenship, but is neccesary for citizenship application.

The PNG Department of Foreign Affairs encouraged refugees to make a decision about permissive residency as soon as possible:

> Assistance from the Government, NGOs [non-government organizations] and UNHCR has been provided to you for many years. However, such assistance cannot continue indefinitely. Before, the only option was voluntary repatriation. You now also have the choice of Permissive Residency. The time has come for you to make a decision … It is in your best interest to apply for one of the above alternatives as soon as possible.[19]

Some people understood that, since permissive residency was renewable at three-yearly intervals, anyone who took the offer would be ineligible to apply for assisted repatriation to Irian Jaya during that three-year period. UNHCR claimed this to be incorrect, and counter to their fundamental principle that voluntary repatriation is always the most desirable durable solution.[20] Without assisted repatriation (provision of an airfare to a person's place of origin in Irian Jaya), most refugees could not afford to return by plane and the difficult terrain could not be traversed otherwise. People understood the following range of options. They could register for assisted repatriation immediately. They could register as permissive residents immediately, and if they changed their minds within three years they could return home as self-funded individuals. Or they could register as permissive residents and if they changed their minds they could join a repatriation programme after three years. Those choosing permissive residency were offered assistance totalling 50 kina per adult and 25 kina per child 'to help improve your living situation at East Awin'.[21] Some referred to the amount as a final payment, completely insufficient for improving their living situation: 'The money is not real money, what can it buy? It can be consumed in a day. Now 1000 kina per person—that might be sufficient to start a small business of some sort.'

Many Muyu perceived their return to be imminent, and had done since their arrival in 1984. The moment of return cannot be reduced to arrangements of identification, registration and international diplomacy. People's decisions were determined by: whether they thought it was safe to return at that time; whether they or their group had achieved what they had set out to; and whether they thought that the new era of political reformation in Indonesia could guarantee their amnesty.

In the event of return, refugees also anticipated their reception by their relatives, neighbours and friends who had not fled. A Biak schoolteacher used a fishing analogy to explain the expectations of family and friends left behind:

> If I plan to go fishing, my family and neighbours observe me preparing my nets and line. They expect me to return with catch, and they expect me to share it with them. If I return empty-handed, they will gossip: 'You are not capable of becoming a fisherman.' We have left behind our families, father, mother and siblings. They have great hope that we will be successful. So, if I return to West Papua before independence, before our goal is achieved, people will protest: 'When will Independence come?' and 'What have you brought home?' We pledged on oath that we would return with result. If we have not yet achieved it, then we must strive until it has been achieved. I will be branded a failure, an ignorant person. I will be rejected. Shame is not evident; I alone will feel it in my heart. But it will become the source of ridicule for many years to come. If there is an event that evokes anger, for example, if my child steals from my neighbour's garden, my neighbour will say: 'Your father

left his garden behind for years, now you steal from mine.' It is later that humiliating words will emerge. If independence is achieved and then we return, our names will be honoured. I may claim: 'I did not go for myself alone but for society.' Whereas if we return without result, we will be considered courageous but it will become a potential source of derision.

Implied in this narrative and similar ones is that repatriation prior to independence signalled the struggle's end—as though there was no longer any purpose in holding out in exile because *merdeka* was not possible. The aphorism: 'who knows if it will be sooner or later' was used by refugees to describe the unknown time of waiting that would hopefully culminate in their return to the homeland. Faith in *merdeka* existed as long as West Papuans remained outside Irian Jaya in protest at Indonesian rule, and in support of political independence. The schoolteacher's narrative elaborates some of the risks to the individual and the collective political struggle in the event of premature return. Educated people claimed that on return their 'civil record', and that of their children, would be negatively affected. Others claimed that they would be involuntarily relocated into transmigration settlements as *translokal*, like people from Weski camp at East Awin had been.

The schoolteacher warned that returnees would be considered courageous, but that the timing of their return (before *merdeka*) would become a 'potential source of derision' and would invoke 'humiliating words'. Premature return would not see repatriates taken in without expectation or obligation. Premature return was also said to betray those who had died in the struggle since crossing to PNG in 1984, and betray the families of the deceased. It was said that if people suddenly appeared 'from nowhere' after 16 years' absence, their relatives and neighbours may suspect the reason for their sudden return. Why had they chosen this moment rather than any other? Some refugees claimed that premature return would release violence. This assertion was based on a notion that West Papuan exile, which allowed access to the outside world, held the key to a relatively peaceable Irian Jaya. Markus's projection of their reception in the event of return and its political effect is illustrative:

We left thinking our flight would produce freedom through world attention. To return now would mean great humiliation in the eyes of our family and in the eyes of the Indonesian government. Upon return, our family will view us as 'guests' and the state will view us as third-class citizens. Indeed, our families live peacefully inside because we are outside. The Indonesian government has kept the peace in order to draw us home. If murders and tortures occur inside, the government knows refugees will not return. Upon our return, the retribution will begin.

Most northerners in support of their nationalist politic conviction intended to avoid repatriation until independence. They spoke of East Awin as an enclave drawing international attention to the struggle for *merdeka*, that is, as a political tactic. This perception was not entirely unfounded. Indonesianist scholars had argued that while the 1984 flight attracted international attention to West Papuan injustices, it also led to a shift in Jakartan representations of the situation in Irian Jaya: the press tried to explain West Papuan grievances, mistakes were acknowledged, government officials visited the province and some intellectuals wrote about the enduring nature of West Papuan nationalism.[22]

In 1997, refugees began registering to become permissive residents. The first batch of applications by West Papuans was intercepted and seized by the landholders at East Awin. According to Bishop Gerard Deschamps of the Daru-Kiunga Diocese, the landholders feared two consequences. First, they feared that the condition of permissive residency allowing resettlement elsewhere in PNG could divest the government of its obligation to compensate them. Second, West Papuan permissive residency applicants who lived outside East Awin were required to relocate to East Awin for six months. The landowners feared that any population increase would further deplete natural resources that had not yet been fully compensated.

Over time, the refugee population also began to fear several consequences arising from their status as permissive residents. Foremost was that they would lose UNHCR's guardianship. As the UNHCR considered an offer of integration by a host government as a 'durable solution', guardianship would no longer be required, resulting in the withdrawal of refugee status to West Papuans. Some refugees pointed out that permissive residency had made their status ambiguous because it appeared to mark a shift towards provisional citizenship. West Papuans had been granted, in principle at least, similar rights and responsibilities to PNG nationals. In theory, the withdrawal of UNHCR guardianship would only occur when refugees obtained full citizenship. To this end protection monitoring activity had continued, with several annual visits by a UNHCR liaison officer. In practice, refugees could list those UNHCR-funded services previously provided at East Awin that had been removed over time. Decline in services and deterioration of infrastructure was apparent. Hospital patients were no longer provided with food and the hospital operated without diesel-powered electricity. Coffins were no longer transported from the camp of the deceased to the cemetery. Fares were introduced on transport from East Awin to the Fly river. Road maintenance halted, sago roofing material was no longer subsidised, correspondence English courses ceased and the secondary school was closed down.

There was a history of resistance to withdrawal of UNHCR services at East Awin. Not surprisingly, these non-violent activities of resistance centred around flags.

As far back as 1993, a demonstration was held in front of the administration building to protest the introduction of transport fares and the termination of other services. Protestors lowered the UN flag and in its place raised the West Papuan flag to full mast, parallel to the PNG flag. The UN flag was raised to full mast on another shorter flagpole, appearing from a distance to be at half-mast. Previously, only the UN and PNG flags had flown parallel at full mast. I was told that the UN flag ought not be flown at full mast if its presence was only half felt. Five leaders were arrested over the protest. In 1996 when the offer of permissive residency was announced, the UN flag was once again lowered and removed.

Some refugees perceived the reduced responsibility of UNHCR evidenced in the decline in services at East Awin as a ploy. It was seen as a ruse by Indonesia and PNG to break refugee resolve to remain in PNG where they were a financial burden, and a continuing embarrassment to Indonesia. The offer of permissive residency functioned as a tactic to compel refugees to eventually register for repatriation. Several times I heard the comment: '[permissive residency] allows survival that's all, until there are those who cannot endure who will request to go home.' In other words, left to their own devices in a hostile PNG economy without UNHCR assistance, West Papuans would be compelled to return to Irian Jaya out of their abject poverty and vulnerability. The Catholic Church of the Daru-Kiunga Diocese and NGOs such as the Austrian Service for Development Cooperation have sought to prevent such a result by providing development assistance, particularly health and education, to the West Papuan refugee population and local landholders.

People at East Awin identified the period 1987–96 as 'the era of the UN'. In contrast, the perception of UNHCR withdrawal beginning in 1997 was seen to augur a new era. Refugees used 'before the UN freed its hands' and 'after the UN freed its hands' as markers of time and prosperity. UNHCR withdrawal was understood by some refugees, in terms of what Malkki has described elsewhere as a 'conjuncture of perceived relations [of collusion] between past and present'.[23] Some refugees believed that UNHCR had 'handed over' administration of West Papuan refugees to PNG. Mindful of history, they drew an analogy with the UN's capitulation to Indonesia that effectively surrendered Netherlands New Guinea to Indonesia. The signing of the New York Agreement in August 1962 by the Netherlands and Indonesia effected a temporary UN administration over Netherlands New Guinea until May 1963. The UN General Assembly ratified the 'unanimous' outcome of the 1969 Act of Free Choice.[24] Both of these events were represented as precedents of UN betrayal and abandonment of West Papuan people.

Refugees tended to read PNG policy towards them over the years as being motivated by a desire to please Indonesia. This was grounded in the perception that Indonesia had actively sought the PNG government's support in repatriating West Papuans since 1984. Ways in which the PNG government was supposed to have encouraged repatriation included: neglect leading to famine in the period 1984–86,[25] relocation to the unsuitable East Awin site in 1987 and threats and acts of deportation. Balancing these perceptions, it ought to be said that PNG is one of the few signatory states of the Refugee Convention in the Pacific region, has initiated the purchase of 6000 hectares at East Awin and has recruited West Papuan teachers and nurses onto the government payroll.

The 1997 permissive residency policy was used by refugees in ways that the Papua New Guinea and Indonesian governments might not have imagined. It could be posited that West Papuan refugees subverted the offers 'by using them with respect to ends and references foreign to the system they had no choice to accept'.[26] In this sense, the uses that they made of permissive residency were tactical. De Certeau's elaboration of tactic allows us to consider the uses or operations of permissive residency by refugees:

> [a tactic] must play on and with a terrain imposed on it and organised by the law of a foreign power. It does not have the means to *keep to itself*, at a distance, in a position of withdrawal, foresight, and self-collection: it is a manoeuvre 'within the enemy's field of vision', ... and within enemy territory. It does not, therefore, have the options of planning a general strategy and viewing the adversary as a whole within a district, visible, and objectifiable space.[27]

De Certeau invites us to look for the difference or similarity between something's production, and the 'secondary production hidden in the process of its utilization'.[28] In the context of permissive residency, I read this as the difference between the permissive residency framework and policy developed by the PNG government and UNHCR, and the refugees' utilisation of permissive residency on the ground. De Certeau says that focusing on processes of utilisation allows us to see the way that a society resists discipline by manipulating the mechanisms of discipline: 'conforming to them only in order to evade them'.[29] The 'operational schema' of tactic is described as intervening in a regulatory field, for example, the application procedure and conditions of permissive residency and repatriation, and introducing a way of turning these regulations to their advantage. By using permissive residency to enable temporary protected return, or relocation to a familiar ecological/cultural landscape, some refugees have utilised the residency law imposed upon them to maintain relations with their own people and place, and sustain their livelihood.

Positing refugees' tactical use of asylum policy implies a certain degree of refugee agency. In doing so, I do not want to negate the sense of profound dilemma in decision-making for many refugees. For those people remaining at East Awin, the future is particularly bleak from the perspective of food production.[30] Most permissive residents cannot afford to relocate outside East Awin, although the terms of their residency permit this. For the majority of West Papuans at East Awin, the weakness of a temporary permissive residency arrangement which is subject to three-yearly renewal is evident. In 2003, the expiry of permits resulted in confusion about the question of renewal and the lack of transparency about the procedure caused anxiety.[31] People whose applications lay waiting to be processed had no legal status, nor did West Papuans who were unable to meet the relocation conditions of permissive residency (i.e., returning temporarily to East Awin). A proposed 2003 PNG Refugee Act offers the promise that processing permissive residency permits can be resolved at a bureaucratic and administrative level. But permissive residents' vulnerability in a hostile PNG economy is also related to domestic political will and economic capacity.

The economic situation for West Papuans at East Awin may radically change in the medium term. The Malaysian timber company GL Niugini Pty Ltd has negotiated a 40-year logging concession with the Awin and Pari landholders of a 200,000 hectare site on the perimeter of the East Awin settlement, close to the Fly River. Planned to commence in mid-2005, the operation would employ as many as 1000 local people to harvest rainforest timber.[32] The labour force would include West Papuans from nearby East Awin as well as local Papua New Guineans retrenched after the OK Tedi mine closure. The entry of cash wages and royalties into the local economy would have a radical impact on the sustainability of livelihoods at East Awin. For those West Papuans who aspire to leave East Awin, harvesting wages may provide the capital necessary for relocation allowed by permissive residency.

Provided the matters of administrative procedures and development assistance can be addressed, the *uses made* of permissive residency suggest benefit. By benefit I mean the production of household wellbeing allowed by freedom of movement to other regions of the host country and the facilitation and maintenance of kin relations allowed by travel between the host country and homeland. These uses of permissive residency allow West Papuan refugees who do not choose repatriation in the short term to move and dwell more comfortably between the homeland and host country. For Gisela and her children, however, the offer of permissive residency offered little comfort. She could not afford to leave East Awin, and neither could she subsist there.[33]

ENDNOTES

[1] cf., Mark Busse, 'Sister exchange among the Wamek of the Middle Fly', PhD thesis, University of California, San Diego, 1987; Mary C. Ayres, 'This side, that side: locality and exogamous group definition in Morehead area, Southwestern Papua', PhD thesis, University of Chicago, 1983.

[2] Klaus Neumann, 'Finding an appropriate beginning for a history of the Tolai colonial past or, starting from trash', *Canberra Anthropology*, 15, 1, 1992, pp. 1–19.

[3] Neumann, 1992, p. 9.

[4] Blaskett, pp. 69; 71.

[5] Article 4 of the 'Basic Agreement between the Government of Papua New Guinea and Government of the Republic of Indonesia on Border Arrangements', Port Moresby, 29 October 1984, cited in E. Wolfers, *Beyond the border, Indonesia and Papua New Guinea*, University of Papua New Guinea Press and The Institute of Pacific Studies, University of the South Pacific, Waigani, PNG, and Suva, Fiji, 1988, p. 164.

[6] Blaskett, p. 69.

[7] Blaskett, p. 231.

[8] Blaskett, p. 247.

[9] Blaskett, p. 246.

[10] Blaskett, pp. 23–5.

[11] Blaskett, pp. 256–309.

[12] Blaskett, pp. 253–4.

[13] International Commission of Jurists, *Status of border crossers*, p. 8.

[14] Ron May, 'East of the border: Irian Jaya and the border in Papua New Guinea's domestic and foreign politics', in R. J. May (ed.), *Between two nations: the Indonesian-Papua New Guinea border and West Papua nationalism*, Robert Brown and Associates, Bathurst, 1986, p. 145.

[15] When signing these instruments, the Government stipulated that 'in accordance with article 42, paragraph 1 of the Convention makes a reservation with respect to the provision contained in articles 17 (1) [wage-earning employment], 21 [Housing], 22 (1) [Public Education], 26 [Freedom of Movement], 31 [Refugees unlawfully in the country of refuge], 32 [Expulsion] and 34 [Naturalisation], of the Convention and does not accept the obligations stipulated in these articles'. (According to the 2003 Joint Report of the International Commission of Jurists and the Refugee Council of Australia ('Seeking refuge: the status of West Papuans in Papua New Guinea', paragraph 305) these reservations reflected the government's concern about the porous nature of the border allowing illegal entry of West Papuans, and concern that the PNG state did not have the economic capacity to grant refugees the same social assistance as PNG citizens.)

[16] Blaskett, pp. 248–9.

[17] International Commission of Jurists and the Refugee Council of Australia, 'Seeking refuge: the status of West Papuans in Papua New Guinea'.

[18] International Commission of Jurists and the Refugee Council of Australia, paragraph 719.

[19] Papua New Guinea Department of Foreign Affairs and Trade, 'Joint UNHCR/PNG Announcement', n.d.

[20] Johann Siffointe, UNHCR Liaison Officer, Port Moresby, pers. comm., November 2004.

[21] Papua New Guinea Department of Foreign Affairs and Trade.

[22] I. Bell., H. Feith and R. Hatley, 'The West Papuan challenge to Indonesian authority in Irian Jaya: old problems, new possibilities', *Asian Survey*, 26, 5, 1986, pp. 539–56.

[23] Malkki, p. 106.

[24] John Saltford, 'United Nations involvement with the act of self determination in West Irian (Indonesian West New Guinea) 1968 to 1969', *Indonesia*, 69, 2000, pp. 71–86.

[25] Kevin Hewison and Alan Smith, '1984: Refugees, "holiday camps" and "deaths"', in R. J. May (ed.), pp. 200–17.

[26] Michel de Certeau, *The practice of everyday life*, University of California, Berkeley, California, 1984, p. xiii.

[27] De Certeau, p. 37.

[28] Original emphasis. De Certeau, p. xiii.

[29] De Certeau, p. xiv.

[30] Robert Askin, 'What is the future for these East Awin children', unpublished report, 2000.

[31] International Commission of Jurists and the Refugee Council of Australia, paragraph 621.

[32] Johann Siffointe, UNHCR Liaison Office Port Moresby, pers. comm., November 2004.

[33] Gisela returned to her border village in 2001.

Chapter 10

Relocation to connected places

I heard news of a raid on East Awin by PNG riot police while waiting at the Kiunga harbour for a connection between motorised canoe travelling on the Fly River and a truck travelling inland to the refugee settlement. Some men who had acted as principal interlocutors in my research had been beaten in the raid. The news deeply disturbed me. I had been away from East Awin for six months, and the raid had occurred three months earlier in December 1998. It was reportedly carried out because of a riot at East Awin, but according to many refugees the riot had been fabricated. The resident policeman had trashed his own station at East Awin to justify a raid on the northerner camp of Waraston. It was rumoured that some West Papuan refugees manufactured weapons and cultivated marijuana to sell to Papua New Guinean thugs known locally as *raskols*. Funds raised were then supposedly used to support activities of the OPM. During the raid, many young men were arrested and detained in the prison in Kiunga. There they slept on flattened cardboard boxes in damp concrete cells, and were required to supply their own food. Providing food was not a simple matter, for their gardens were located at East Awin. The journey between Kiunga and East Awin was not scheduled, and depending on the weather, could take 12 hours or several days. The cost of a tractor or truck and motorised canoe was set at about 35 kina for a return journey. When I heard news of the raid at the harbour that day, the men from East Awin had already been detained without trial in Kiunga jail for three months.

At East Awin, the police had trashed and looted several kiosks owned by refugees and incinerated two houses. Women hid with young children in the Immanuel Church, and buried household items in the rainforest, fearing that their houses would be burned down. Young men were the target of the operation and they sought cover in the forest on the margins of the settlement. One of the houses burned had been built by a nurse called Fabian and his wife Katrine in time for the arrival of their third child. During the raid, Fabian attempted to mediate an armed conflict between the riot police and refugees at Waraston camp. The deliberate burning of Fabian's house as retribution was the subject of everyday conversation at East Awin in the following months. A house was said to contain a family's spirit. To have one's house burned or destroyed was to leave behind part of one's spirit. Commenting on the destruction of his son-in-law Fabian's house, Leonardo explained that a house was built on the sweat of its owner: 'According to [Leonardo's north coast] custom, my house mirrors myself, my body. I do not burn my own skin. This house has been built by my own sweat that has been shed.' The analogy 'my house is like myself' was also pragmatic, for to be without shelter and without tools and cooking implements was to be destitute. The destruction of Fabian and Katrine's house relativised the experience of displacement at East Awin. The community were confronted with another dimension of displacement, of losing their houses and belongings in a place of 'refuge'.

Northerners read the police raid, referred to colloquially as the 'December incident', in terms of a foreboding future. The December incident illustrated their vulnerability as permissive residents. Their reading was not without foundation—even the US Refugee Committee commented that: 'UNHCR no longer considers persons with permissive residency … to be refugees', because the status 'is a durable solution which grants recipients similar rights and responsibilities to those of PNG nationals'.[1] Some northerners explained the December incident in terms of allegory. Their treatment by police members during the raid was congruous with a previous experience in 1988, when their church had been burned to the ground to force their relocation to East Awin.[2]

From 1984, all northerners had lived together at Blackwater camp near Vanimo. After a factional split occurred, a group of about 200 northerners left Blackwater and established a camp at Pasi Beach, to the east of Vanimo. The PNG government wanted to relocate all northerner West Papuans living proximate to the border to East Awin. Blackwater camp residents were suspected of collusion with OPM fighters in several incidents. In 1988, an OPM raid was carried out on an Indonesian transmigration camp at Arso, south west of Vanimo, and hostages were taken and released. Subsequently, about 200 Indonesian soldiers crossed the international border into PNG to raid a camp that was said to contain those involved in the Arso raid.[3] It was also claimed that 90 West Papuans had deserted Blackwater camp along with an OPM leader to resume guerrilla activity in the border area.[4] Commentators suggested that the Indonesian government had pressed the PNG government to close Blackwater camp, claiming that refugee involvement in the attack contravened the terms of the International Border Agreement.[5]

Refugees at Blackwater appealed to the UNHCR not to be resettled at East Awin. A petition with 300 signatures was sent to the UN, the PNG government, and international NGOs. The petition protested relocation to East Awin on several grounds. At Blackwater, refugees had established houses, productive gardens and good relations with the local landholders. They claimed that a large-scale camp would render them vulnerable to aerial bombardment, and there would be difficulty integrating refugees of different ethnicity.[6] Refugees from Blackwater were eventually relocated to East Awin in 1988, but the northerners at Pasi beach resisted being moved.

From East Awin, Pasi beach refugees recalled their former beachside camp as utopic. At night they had been able to trace car headlights winding slowly around the headland to the capital Jayapura. The headlights guided them mnemonically to the place from which they had fled, allowing a kind of panopticon. They could see their homes in the distance from a position of darkened cover. The familiar coastal environment allowed prosperity. They practised commercial fishing, even purchasing outboard motors to assist their catch. Women baked cakes and breads to sell in the Vanimo market. They played basketball and soccer with the locals, and attended each other's church services. In Appadurian terms they had 'produced locality' among their group and with the landholders, and they had no desire to relocate to East Awin. Unlike refugees' perception of the Awin landholders, northerners viewed their relation with the landholder Ninggra in terms of mutual exchange.

A UNHCR briefing document stated that: 'refugees who refused to move to East Awin in 1988 were forced by the [PNG] Government in December 1989 to move to East Awin camp using the new provisions under the amended Migration Act'.[7] The act of forcing northerner refugee relocation to East Awin involved the burning of their Immanuel Protestant Church. According to the witnessing congregation, this was carried out by police under PNG government order. The incident occurred during an operation which saw government officials mobilise and transport the Immanuel congregation by aeroplane from their beachside settlement near Vanimo to the inland UNHCR settlement at East Awin. Relocation of the Immanuel congregation was the last in a series of exercises to resettle West Papuan refugees from informal border camps to a single site at East Awin. The rationale of relocation centred around improved service provision, enhanced food security and prospects for self-sufficiency, and segregation of refugees from the local population and military activity in the border region.[8]

The burning of the church was recounted by several northerners. It is represented textually below as a compilation narrative, drawn mainly from the account of a senior congregation member who witnessed the burning of the church. Further details have been inserted from narratives of the same event recounted by three other congregation members:

> Between September and December 1989 we were watched by police. The police prohibited us associating with people outside of our camp. They coaxed the older Ninggra people [landholders] to evict us from the land they had given us. The Ninggra people then ordered us to build a canoe to carry 200 people. Ninggra people only know how to build small canoes called *kole-kole*. Whereas we are renowned for building large ocean outriggers. We built two canoes for them. One named Morning Star, the other Wintimbas II. We understood the canoe to be a sort of guarantee for us on Ninggra land. Around this time Bernard Narakobi advised the

Ninggra that West Papuan people were a blessing but if neglected would leave this place and take with them their blessing.[9] In December the police brought dogs. They were afraid we would resist. We already knew their plan. We had said to them: 'We are not thieves, why are you forcing us to leave?' The women had prepared fried fish and small cakes. Upon the police arrival we invited them to eat. The aroma was enticing. They could not force us to leave after that. The following day we prepared food again. Then the sea became rough and we could not catch fish. Instead, we gave a cuscus skin to the Police Commander, a Hagen man. We captured that cuscus in the tree that we felled for our church's foundation pillar. So, he commanded his unit not to use dogs or weapons or wear uniforms. For two weeks there was no action. Some police were Seventh Day Adventists. They opposed the command to burn our houses, and retreated from duty. They had observed us gathering to pray each morning and feared for their own salvation if they harmed us. Finally in December, the church was lit. We were sitting inside the church praying at the time. The police turned up their vehicle radios to drown out our prayers. A congregation leader scooped soil from around the base of the foundation pillar and holding it skywards pronounced: 'We have been evicted with violence. You must act upon this injustice.' We abandoned the church. We did not wish to see it burn. Upon reaching Vanimo we turned to see the smoke. Later a nun fetched two charred pieces to form a cross for the new church.

To understand the impact on the Immanuel congregation, we need to consider the meaning given to 'the church' by those West Papuans who represent themselves as culturally and authentically Christian.[10] Among West Papuan Christian congregations, faith in God is integral to a discourse of *merdeka* or political independence. Faith in *merdeka* is inextricably tied to Christian faith: people conceive independence as a state that will be brought about by God's intervention. Refugees at East Awin often referred to the books of Genesis and Exodus to demonstrate the territorialised nature of nations. For example, it was claimed that the Bible legend of the flood in Genesis (10) substantiated a Muyu legend of Creation about the territorialisation of nations: in the beginning all people evolved from the island of New Guinea, but when the flood came only Papuans could stay on Papuan land, and other races were carried away to other islands. The book of Exodus was paraphrased as a motif about 'people's yearning to return to or re-possess their place: every human being yearns for their land of birth.' Plainly the emphasis here is on nativism—an almost primordial attachment to a geographical place of origin.

West Papuan theologian and anthropologist Benny Giay has described the church as an emancipatory institution: a pillar or buffer in the journey of the West

Papuan nation, and a last bastion bringing new hope to a people faced with a rigid state order.[11] Giay says that West Papuan people hear the Bible according to what they want to hear, and the church both absorbs peoples' aspirations for freedom and is itself a source of inspiration based on a perception that God supports liberation. The Bible allows congregations to imagine a world free of trickery and sorcery, intimidation and trauma. It offers a window onto another world identified by some as a liberated West Papua.

Significantly, West Papuan refugee congregations at East Awin built churches even before they had built their own houses. They gathered in these churches almost daily to read the Bible, sing gospel and pray together. In spite of the religiously inflected struggle for *merdeka*, some congregation members disapproved of the church used as a meeting place. Political meeting that inevitably produced quarrelling was categorised as profane activity. Where a place such as a church is designated sacred through the presence of certain objects like an altar or tabernacle, then actions that are considered to be profane in character are prohibited in that place.

In the process of building the Immanuel Church, congregation members participated in certain rituals to render sacred or en-spirit the building made by men. A ceremony was held at the time that the foundation post was planted. Bible readings were conducted, and congregation members buried money and gifts with the foundation post. These offerings were said to engage God's blessing of the church and congregation. At the time that the church was burned, retrieval of soil from the foundation post symbolically recalled this history of sacrifice. So too did the earlier gifting of the cuscus to the police commander, for its tree of origin was the church's foundation post.

Following the burning of the church and their forced relocation, the congregation built a new church at East Awin and named it Immanuel. In 1998, a tenth anniversary of the Immanuel Church at East Awin commemorated the desecration of the original church. A lay preacher—himself an Immanuel congregation member—explained that both Immanuel churches had been built before people had built their own houses. He read a Bible passage from Revelations (21:3) which had also been read at the time of the planting of the original Immanuel foundation post: 'And I heard a loud voice from the throne saying, see, the home of God is among mortals. He will dwell with them as their God they will be his peoples, and God himself will be with them.' The preacher recalled that the Immanuel congregation had built a place to worship God inspired by Jacob's revelation in Genesis. He recounted the dream in which Jacob received a revelation about salvation and God's presence in exile: 'Know that I am with you and will keep you wherever you go, and will bring you back to this land; for I will not leave you until I have done what I have promised you' (Genesis 28:20–22). The Immanuel congregation at East Awin read into Jacob's revelation a kind of teleology of return to the geographical West Papuan homeland. Return to the homeland was destined, and tied to faith in God. And faith in God was most obviously demonstrated by the act of building a church before one's own home.

Photo 5. Decorated wall, entry area of house at Waraston camp, East Awin.

Photo: Diana Glazebrook.

The combination of church burning and forced relocation was interpreted by the Immanuel refugee congregation in terms of a discourse of suffering and liberation. The burning of the church had occurred in a place of apparent refuge. At the time, PNG had ratified the UN Refugee Convention and had recognised West Papuan asylum seekers as refugees (albeit with substantial reservations in relation to wage-earning, education, freedom of movement, expulsion and naturalisation).[12] The burning of the church was reportedly carried out by government officials, who, according to my interlocutors, ought to have acted as protectors in a place established as a refuge. Some refugees interpreted the circumstances of their relocation to East Awin as a covert effort by the PNG and Indonesian governments to break their spirit, compelling their repatriation back to Irian Jaya. At the time, it was viewed as the most recent in a litany of events of suffering endured by West Papuans in the homeland, and now in PNG. It acted to substantiate their sense of categorical injustice, and girded their faith in God to assist bringing about West Papuan freedom imagined as *merdeka*. It also deepened refugee distrust in the aspirations of the PNG government, for such a deliberate act of desecration was thought to have been orchestrated by Indonesia.

More than any other event occurring in the period of exile, including the burning of the Immanuel Church, the December incident was cathartic. Northerners had previously given much significance to the idea of East Awin as a united West Papuan refugee enclave attracting international attention. During the raid, northerners were the targets of police interrogation and punishment, while the rest of the population—according to northerners—were 'ambivalent' onlookers. The raid effected a very disillusioned nadir in northerners, altering their resolve to endure exile at East Awin. Some planned to leave East Awin and relocate to a coastal environment that resembled their own place. The new status of permissive residency while affecting UNHCR-derived forms of material support, also allowed them to leave East Awin.

Some northerners planned to use the permissive residency laws imposed on them to dwell more comfortably, allowing them to sustain what they see as their political exile. Permissive residency allows relocation elsewhere in PNG and temporary return to the homeland. Each adult has been issued with an identification form and passport photo known as a permission letter. Among West Papuan refugees, permissive residency identification papers were conceived as 'passports' allowing return to the homeland to visit their relatives and family. It was claimed that the papers identified them as provisional PNG citizens, as inter-national subjects. Displayed in the Indonesian Province of Papua, permissive residency status is deemed protective, while in PNG it is perceived as discriminatory. People mentioned plans to return to their parents' or sibling's home for a particular occasion like Christmas or Easter, before returning again to PNG. Such a return journey is embraced by Casey's explanations of 'homecoming' as a journey that may involve a return trip back to one's contemporary home.[13] At a physical distance the homeland may be recalled as an 'unproblematic geographic location' which is familiar.[14] Yet a return trip may bring disillusion, and events that have occurred since October 2001 in the renewed campaign to crush independence may have inflected the homeland with terror once more.

The prospect of leaving East Awin to relocate to a coastal environment was an ecstatic one for northerners. But most could not afford the plane ticket out of Kiunga to get to the coast and the mountainous route cannot be traversed otherwise. In theory at least, the conditions of permissive residency enable relocation to an environment that can sustain people's livelihoods. While the inland, isolated East Awin site was considered to be a place characterised by deprivation, the north coast—also a place of refuge inside PNG—was remembered by northerners in almost idyllic terms. The setting sun at East Awin invoked a coastal landscape for Luther: 'When the sun sets here, I am reminded of watching the setting of the sun there. I remember the trees radiant in its glow, and fish playing on the water's surface. I remember my place with deep sorrow.' This familiar coastal environment was the most recent memory and experience of a prosperous home, and the only memory for most school-aged children.

Those who have afforded to take advantage of relocation so far have done so in small groups, relocating with several kinsmen or people from the same region to places that are *connected* to the homeland. These connected places are serviced by transport such as minibus and boat, and public telephone facilities. Connected places enable real and virtual contact with the homeland village. Relocation to a connected place means that in spite of the border, social relations with kin and neighbours in homeland villages of origin can be resumed and sustained. The opportunity to resume or generate a new social space across borders resonates with an Appadurian notion of 'translocality',[15] and Velayutham and Wise's application of translocal to the village level offers particular insight.[16] They show the social practices, responsibilities and obligations of a certain community outside the homeland to be exclusively oriented to the small-scale place from where the community originated. In the 'translocal village', two places across borders might come to be connected at the level of the everyday by 'material, family, social, symbolic networks and exchanges'.

For 14 years the sheer isolation of East Awin effectively disconnected northerner and highlander refugees from their homeland villages and regions. In the relocation of small groups of kin or neighbours from East Awin to places elsewhere in PNG that are connected to the homeland, there is the opportunity for new social spaces to be generated—both in the new place of relocation and between this new place and the homeland village or region. Re-entry into material, family and social networks and exchanges, enabled by permissive residency, may serve to anchor people's sociality in spite of their location outside the homeland.

ENDNOTES

[1] US Committee for Refugees, 'Papua New Guinea: World Refugee Survey 2003 Country Report', <http://www.refugees.org/world/countryrpt/easia_pacific/2003/papua_new_guinea.cfm>.

[2] Diana Glazebrook, 'Desecration in a place of refuge', *Cultural Studies Review*, 11, 1, 2005, pp.98–109.

[3] Blaskett, p. 308.

[4] Hastings, p. 228.

[5] Preston, pp. 865–6.

[6] *West Papuan Observer*, 9, 3, 1984, pp. 7–8.

[7] United Nations High Commission for Refugees, 'Additional background information on the [East Awin] project', Canberra, 1993.

[8] Preston, p. 231.

[9] A former member of parliament, Narakobi is a renowned human rights lawyer and outspoken advocate of the legal rights of West Papuan refugees.

[10] J. Barker, 'Mission station and village: cultural practice and representations in Maisin society', in J. Barker (ed.), *Christianity in Oceania: ethnographic perspectives*.

[11] Giay, pp. 59–63.

[12] When signing these instruments, the PNG government stipulated that 'in accordance with article 42, paragraph 1 of the Convention makes a reservation with respect to the provision contained in articles

17 (1) [wage-earning employment], 21 [Housing], 22 (1) [Public Education], 26 [Freedom of Movement], 31 [Refugees unlawfully in the country of refuge], 32 [Expulsion] and 34 [Naturalisation], of the Convention and does not accept the obligations stipulated in these articles' (http://untreaty.un.org).

[13] Casey, *Getting back into place*, p. 291.

[14] Gow, pp. 4–5.

[15] Appadurai, p. 192.

[16] Selvaraj Velayutham and Amanda Wise, 'Moral economies of a translocal village: obligation and shame among South Indian Transnational Migrants', *Global Networks*, 3, 1, 2005, pp. 27–47.

Chapter 11

Being 'indigenous' in the Indonesian province of Papua

Lina was selling individual pieces of cutlery on a piece of hessian sacking in the East Awin market when we first met. As I passed by her in my search for chillis, she tugged at my billum. Woven from natural fibres and dyed with local pigments, the billum was one I had bought in Wamena, West Papua. From her seated position Lina pulled the billum to her body, and burying her face in it, inhaled deeply: 'O', she cried, 'I can smell the soil of my place in this billum.' I explained to Lina that I had bought it in the market in Wamena, and invited her to view the photographs of my trip. The photographs of the Baliem Valley landscape, of cultivated plots bordered with streams and neat sapling fences and Dani women selling vegetables in the marketplace, invoked great excitement in Lina, and her women friends Griet, Josina and Elsje. They seemed unfussed by the photographs that documented the domination of the Wamena market by migrants. Bugis and Madurese owned most of the small eating stalls or *warung*, as well as the kiosks, and larger shops around the marketplace. I learned from Lina and her friends that they were selling their meagre possessions in the East Awin market because they were on the brink of return to Wamena.

Lina and her friends carried out their preparations for repatriation clandestinely. They were aware that others viewed their repatriation to be premature, and usually travelled to the camp of their leader, an evangelical lay preacher from the north coast, under the cover of dawn or dusk. Other refugees knew indirectly of Dani people's planned repatriation through activities like the sale of cutlery and other small household items in the marketplace, and the sale of houses for demolition. The actual date of repatriation was a matter of secrecy. Some spoke about the need to burn their houses in their wake, fearing that their personal traces could be used as the substance of sorcery or magic against them.

In July 1998, I attended a religious service in the Wamena Baptist Church at East Awin to farewell repatriating Dani. In many ways it was like any other service: hibiscus and bouganvillea had been placed in vases at the door, and people sang hymns in pidgin with gusto in spite of the mangy dogs that fought each other in the back stalls of the church. Unlike other congregations at East Awin that used texts in Indonesian, the Wamena congregation used Bibles and songbooks in pidgin. Most Dani adults had learned to read and write at East Awin, but in pidgin. They could speak basic Indonesian, but were not literate in it. On the morning of the farewell, the service began with the testimonials of male congregation members who recounted their involvement with the OPM since 1969. Some speakers concluded that military strategy had not produced results, and that they had gained nothing. Josina's husband spoke dramatically of the Israelites who had lived in the desert for 40 years—the period of one generation—circling continuously when the path home was short. He then asked the congregation: 'Will you also circle aimlessly when the path home is short, will your fate be the same?' For months the farewell event had been mentioned as an opportunity to shake the hands of fellow Dani who had chosen not to repatriate. Men shook hands, and sought forgiveness from one another for past words and actions arising from their different political allegiances. Privately, returnees said they felt the contempt of those staying, and it was said that the dogs of repatriating Dani left behind at East Awin would be renamed 'returned' or 'surrendered', as a matter of ridicule. In the absence of their owners, these dogs reminded people that repatriation amounted to surrender, or yielding to the Indonesian state.

At the time of the farewell in 1998, about 200 Dani people lived in two camps at East Awin, named Wamena I and Wamena II. Residence in either camp was determined by political allegiance, specifically, whether one supported the military strategy of the OPM or not. The two camps merged for social events such as church services, prayer groups, literacy classes and funerals. Most Dani at East Awin shared with Katarina (Chapter 3) the journey of flight from the Baliem to Mamberamo to the border. At East Awin, Dani composed songs in Indonesian and Dani languages that invoked the name Wamena and the Baliem Valley landscape. The songs intensify states of loss and sorrow felt by Dani as a result of living outside their homeland. These feeling states are central to the evocative nature of the songs. The six songs below appear like verses of a single song, but are actually discrete songs. Categorised as 'songs of sadness', they are sung to invoke weeping during the period before the burial of a deceased person and 40 days after burial. The songs comprise a single line lyric or verse repeated almost meditatively, with the harmony changing slightly after several sets of repetition:

First song:
Pity, Wamena is already faraway
Children, don't cry.

Second song:
Father, Mother, look over there
The clouds keep rolling in.

Third song:
O! Friends we feel hungry, our place is faraway
Friends can you give us food?

Fourth song:
How is Wamena: is it far or close?
The mountain and the cape are hidden.

Fifth song:
The children they question their father and mother
Is our village distant or close by?

Sixth song:
When will we return to see our homeland?
It is so long since we left our village

The second song refers to the sighting of high, rolling white clouds to the west of East Awin. This familiar cloud formation recalls their highland place, and villages and relatives left behind. The third song was composed in Indonesian by Dani children whose parents fled the Baliem Valley in 1977, and recalls their starvation at various times during the journey of flight. The fourth song refers to Dani children born outside the Baliem, who only know the location of Wamena and its glory through the stories of their parents.

In 1977, Griet, Elsje and Josina walked together with several hundred other Dani from the Baliem Valley northwards over the mountains, descending into the swampy lowlands of Mamberamo. In 1983, they set out again to walk eastwards from Mamberamo to PNG. Elsje's husband Justus explained to me that many Dani people had perished in the course of these two journeys. In the event of repatriation, those Dani who survived were responsible for explaining the deaths of those who had not. Or at least, those who survived had to return with some sort of advantage that could justify the deprivations of the deceased. Justus's ascetism practised at East Awin remembered the death of his parents and siblings in the Baliem Valley in 1977. Since fleeing, Justus had not worn shoes and had not shaved as a sign of grief. He claimed that upon his return, his brother would take pity and buy him a pair of shoes. Then in a public ceremony, his brother would place Justus's feet in those shoes and cut his beard. It was not only Justus who embodied his grief. Other men who fled, leaving behind wives and children, had not re-married. Nor had wives, and children had delayed marriage in honour of absent fathers.

Justus's resolve was steeled by the memory of kin whose lives had been sacrificed. To return to the homeland before any outcome had been achieved diminished the sacrifice of those who had died. To endure exile was to repay their sacrifice, to uphold their honour. In order to return, it was necessary to do so with *hasil*, meaning 'success' or 'result' in Indonesian. Losses sustained had to be compensated. Defending his decision to repatriate, Justus explained that it was founded on his membership of a group called the West Papuan Indigenous People's Association, known by the acronym WPIA. It was the articulation of 'indigeneity', and the use of indigeneity as a political identity, that Justus conceived as an object or result. Previously, Justus and other WPIA members had little if any conception of themselves as belonging to a global category of indigenous or 'fourth world' peoples whose land had been appropriated by colonial governments. Drawing on a discourse of indigeneity, WPIA members claimed that international recognition of themselves as indigenous would privilege them in relation to 'newcomers' i.e., migrants. They defined indigenous as a 'native' or 'original' person able to trace their descent in a particular place, and in categorical opposition to people who had recently arrived from somewhere else.

In an interview published in the Jayapura-based tabloid *Jubi* (short for *jujur bicara* or literally 'speaking frankly' or 'straight talk' in Indonesian), a WPIA member elaborated indigeneity:

> We fled leaving behind our places of origin because here [Irian Jaya] people did not value our rights as indigenous citizens. Now we have returned and want to carry on the struggle for our rights which are directly protected by the UN … And now we have returned to the land of our origin … We have returned not out of hunger or thirst or difficulties of survival. But, now indeed is already the time for us to return. Why? We think for what [purpose] should we exist outside and demand our rights from outside? What we demand here is the fairness and honesty of the government in seeing to the interests of Papuan people. Not just as a demand for independence, but how Papuans are developed and assisted. This was our thinking and reason for our return …[1]

WPIA evolved from the 1993 UN Year of Indigenous People. A transnational alliance of indigenous people facilitated by a secretariat in Geneva, its slogan 'peace, human rights, democracy' struck a chord with West Papuan refugees who rejected military means. An evangelical pastor at East Awin called Jeronimus, himself a refugee, received mail from the UN Secretariat, and subsequently established WPIA. Jeronimus positioned himself as leader, and promoted indigenous identity as a means to claim privileges in relation to migrants, especially in the matter of land rights. The following extract is taken from another interview in *Jubi* with a WPIA returnee in the month of his return:

> We are not transmigrants or translocals. We are refugees. We are not people who have fled in order to look for a place. But we have returned to our homeland. So, we are people who have left behind the place of our homeland and returned again to our home village … It is we who have a place, have a homeland. We are not transmigrants. We are indigenous inhabitants. So, where is the government attention towards

us? What we request is that the government sees to the interests of indigenous Papuan inhabitants.[2]

Members were well versed on the subject of indigeneity, and in the course of everyday conversation, spoke knowledgeably about International Labor Organisation (ILO) Conventions 107 and 169 relating to indigenous and tribal peoples. It seems unlikely that Jeronimus informed his constituency that the Indonesian government had refused to ratify the UN's Indigenous and Tribal People's Convention, and had legislated against the concept of indigeneity in Presidential Decree No. 26/1998: 'stopping the use of the term Indigenous and Non-Indigenous in all formulations, policy implementations, program planning and activity implementation and government policy'.[3] The entry of the concept of SARA (an acronym in Indonesian referring to ethnicity, religion, race, class) into Indonesian discourse is not coincidental. The privileging of a particular category in relation to another is considered discriminatory, and any 'claim' based on one's membership in a certain category such as ethnic, religious or racial, can be discredited by invoking SARA. In short, to claim rights based on indigeneity is considered discriminatory against those who are not indigenous.

The UN Secretariat produced generic paraphernalia that was ascribed different meanings at the local level. Some WPIA members claimed that the logos of the UN and International Year of Indigenous People stencilled onto t-shirts and jerseys gave protective powers to wearers. Shielded by these marked pieces of clothing, it was said that WPIA members had travelled safely back and forth across the international border. WPIA posters showing the UN logo had allegedly been pasted across Irian Jaya, but were neither torn down nor defaced. International connections were claimed to bear witness and afford protection. Justus grounded the power of these logos in the rationale of international politics: Indonesia did not want to damage its relationship with the US-dominated UN and its institutions. Other WPIA members attributed a kind of supernatural agency to UN paraphernalia like logos—as though they were enspirited.

Jeronimus selected dates carefully to coincide with historical events in which West Papua figured. For example, he selected the original date of WPIA members' planned repatriation for 15 August 1998. This day commemorated US General Macarthur's Proclamation of Peace ending World War II, announced from Jayapura (then Hollandia) in 1945. According to Justus, West Papuan victimisation by the Japanese in support of the American allies during the Second World War had rendered the US morally indebted to West Papua. Justus admitted that Jeronimus and WPIA members were on their own in thinking that this event was significant. Other West Papuans derided the idea, claiming it to be 'trash': an event that led nowhere and offered no basis for a political claim in the present. Jeronimus sought out opportunities to raise the West Papuan flag alongside other national flags in an inter-national formation. He even planned for the repatriation to be launched by a ceremony in which the flags of America, Japan, PNG, and West Papua would be flown in parallel. Like the UN logo, national flags were considered to have a sort of human agency, or witnessing capacity: 'Others don't want to return home with us. They say they are afraid to die. If the Indonesians want to kill us while we are standing on top of these flags, so be it.' It was said that Jeronimus had invited Indonesia's President Habibie, PNG Prime Minister Skate, and UN peacekeepers to attend the launch of their repatriation.

Jeronimus was hailed as a Moses figure by his WPIA constituency:

> In the story of Exodus, through the prophet Moses, God performed ten miracles of plagues and still Pharoah was hard hearted, refusing to let the Israelis out of Egypt. The Israelis were slaves. Suharto was like Pharaoh. Jeronimus is a prophet and deliverer like Moses. As we have seen from the history of Israel, Moses led them home. West Papuan people can similarly be saved. (Justus)

At Jeronimus's camp at East Awin, WPIA members built a monument dedicated to Psalm 23 'The Lord is my Shepherd' and the principle of tithe. Tithe was enshrined in the 'charters' of each of the three main political alliances at East Awin. The principle of tithe recognised that *merdeka* would only be achieved through God's intervention (i.e., Lord as Shepherd), and that following independence, a tithe of 10 per cent of state income would support the work of God in the new state.

WPIA members were also influenced by the ideas of a Dutch pastor named Leenhout. His sermon was translated into Indonesian by a West Papuan living in exile in the Netherlands and since 1986 had been distributed to West Papuans in PNG. A schoolteacher at East Awin explained Leenhout's revelation to me. In 1948, the pastor apparently received divine revelations relating to Romans 9 and 11, and Ephesians 2:11–22 in the New Testament. The revelation occurred at the time of two significant events, both involving Israel. First, at the formation of the World Council of Churches its membership included churches that did not recognise Jesus as Messiah. Second, Israel's constitution as a political state denied its non-secular nature as Promised Land. Leenhout preached that Israel was a window through which God viewed the world but while Israel remained a political state, peace would elude the world. God had intentionally hardened the heart of Jews so that Christ's teachings would be spread to other nations. The salvation of black colonised nations, including West Papua, was said to be wrapped up in the fate of Israel, and it was the responsibility of the peoples of these nations to evangelise Israel.

In fact, Leenhout's sermon made scant reference to West Papua. So we might deduce that the West Papuan translator, himself a pastor, as well as congregation leaders and followers at East Awin, have interpreted Leenhout in light of their own theological and political standpoints. Leenhout rejects military retaliation and preaches repentance and surrender of the struggle into God's hands. Critics of Leenhout claim that preaching surrender plays into the hands of the Indonesian state. In a 1998 Christmas sermon posted to East Awin, the translated sermon mentioned the government of Israel's plea for members of the Jewish diaspora to return to Israel to help develop their nation. WPIA leaders interpreted this sermon analogously as a call for West Papuans to return to Irian Jaya to assist develop the nation-state, rather than return in its wake. The idea of connection between Irian Jaya and Israel may have been influenced by a publication titled *From Jerusalem to Irian Jaya* which had been advertised and reviewed in the Catholic weekly *Tifa Irian*, a newspaper that occasionally circulated at East Awin.[4] While I knew of no copies of the book at East Awin and knew of no-one who had read the book, many people referred to its title.

While Jeronimus planned the repatriation of his group prior to the millennium, the event finally took place in 2000. As I had left East Awin in 1999, I have no evidence of the way Jeronimus related the timing of repatriation to the new millennium. Given his propensity for reading signs though, it is probable that he represented the new millennium as an historical juncture—a new era for West Papuans. Like many other Christians the world over, Jeronimus might have believed that entry into the third millennium would mark Christ's return, and the liberation of the world's colonised peoples. This premonition circulated among some congregations of the Daru-Kiunga Diocese which included East Awin and the border camps. The decision made by Indonesia's President Abdurrahman Wahid to spend 31 December 1999 in Jayapura, heightened speculation about West Papua's future in the new millennium. The state's intransigence on the question of *merdeka* can also be read into the time and place of Wahid's visit. In other words, Indonesia's future in the new millennium rests on Irian Jaya's continued incorporation in the Republic. The Bishop's pragmatic letter to the Daru-Kiunga Diocese counselled against heeding false prophets:

> Actually what will happen in the Year 2000? The sun will rise in the morning as usual and will set on dusk as usual. Everything will continue as today. People's lives will not change. Good people will continue to be good. Evil people will continue their habits, which are evil. The bells will continue to summon people to church to hear God's utterance. The government and businesses will continue to work for development. Rural congregations will continue to work in their gardens. The society will continue to experience various difficulties and problems, like now. But several people will discover new problems, that is, those who want to listen to false prophets. There are those who will stop work in their gardens, others will abandon their jobs. They will use up their food and money. There are people who will withdraw all of their money from the

bank and waste it on food and drink for the final party. After that they will regret because they have spent all of their money. Other people will gather in the one place together and wait for judgement day. But judgement day will not come and they will have finished their food and anger will emerge among them. Many sorts of propaganda and crusades will end without fulfilling any promise or result whatsoever.

The Bishop's sober counsel offers insight into millenarian thinking. In the case of Irian Jaya, millenarianism emerges where development projects do not fulfil their promises, persistent corruption occurs in the bureaucracy, land is appropriated and re-settlement enforced, and West Papuans consider themselves to be treated as less than human.[5] Collective sentiments of disappointment, distrust, and humiliation can bring to the surface individuals who claim to have received revelations about the resolution of economic and political discontent.

It was the entry into what was perceived as a new era that left people vulnerable to the rumour of *merdeka*'s imminence—that West Papua would become a nation-state, and that those in exile had been summoned home. Kirsch describes millennialism as a globalising discourse, synchronising a people's fate. Millennialism attributes the power to bring about change 'to an abstract moment of time, which is by definition independent of place' and ignores prior location of power in the landscape and other beings inhabiting that place.[6] Faith in *merdeka* becomes millennial when the moment of its occurrence is predicted, but faith in *merdeka* that will occur more abstractly at some time in the future is not millennial. Benny Giay has described West Papuan conceptions of Indonesian occupation as the latest in a sequence or episodes or stages, beginning with Papuans ruling their own land, followed by the arrival of Christian missionaries from the West and consecutive colonial occupations (Dutch, Japanese, Indonesian).[7] According to this schema, the episode following Indonesian occupation will be *merdeka*. The final episode will be marked by the arrival of Christ. Giay's point is that the incorporation of West Papua into the Indonesian Republic is one episode that has been preceded by and will be succeeded by other episodes.

In the period 1998–99, approximately 1000 people at East Awin registered for repatriation. In spite of people's hopes for the millennium and the offer of assisted repatriation in a millenial year, less than one-sixth of East Awin refugees (632) joined the repatriation operation that took place in September 2000. Very few registered for repatriation as individuals. Those registering were mainly members of WPIA who claimed that the offer of assisted repatriation allowed their passage home in order to assist in the development of their nation from the inside. During the period of decision-making, Jeronimus constantly postponed the timing of repatriation. Some WPIA members confided in me that so many delays had occurred that they doubted whether it would actually take place.

Lina registered for repatriation, along with Elsje, Josina and Griet. When I first met Lina in the market when she was selling her cutlery, I assumed she was pregnant. I learned instead that she suffered from a distended spleen due to persistent malaria and had chronic anaemia. Several times she had refused to travel to Kiunga for treatment for a bad bout of malaria because she felt too weak to make the journey. One morning, a neighbour returned from the morning market with the news that Lina had died. The neighbour was not surprised—she claimed to have seen Lina's spirit, which had already left her body, at the market two days prior. Elsje described to me how Lina's seven-year-old son had tended Lina's deathbed, cleaning her when she could not wash herself. Lina had left a message that she did not want a coffin, instead she wanted to be buried in her kitchen cupboard. Her body was laid in a state of wake for a day and a night, propped up on blankets in a half-lying position and festooned with a dozen or more coloured billum. It was the timing of her parting which was heart-breaking for Elsje, Josina and Griet: after 21 years they were finally returning to their place, without Lina. Their euphoric return would be affected by the fact that Lina would remain at East Awin. Lina's burial connected her friends to East Awin, and in the period after her death they viewed departure with ambivalence. The eulogy for Lina was a litany of departures and separations: separation from her husband after his flight in 1977, prolonged detention by Indonesian soldiers following this event, forsaking her young daughter to travel to Jayapura where she walked on foot to the border to be reunited with her husband, the death of her second-born child on her arrival to East Awin in 1987, and finally, leaving behind two young boys aged three and seven.

Lamentations sung at Lina's wake recalled her flight from the Baliem Valley and mourned her premature departure. For Dani, a lamentation known as *lendawe* is a eulogy that speaks of the past when the deceased lived, and imagines the future in the absence of the deceased. Usually *lendawe* connects the deceased to their place of origin: their village, mountain and river, as well as their close kin. In spite of its improvised character, *lendawe* must be sung with care to avoid offending the deceased's relatives. *Lendawe* increases in intensity at the time when night enters dawn on the day of burial. Sitting around the deceased, people think: this is the last day we will see their face, the last day we will meet—tomorrow we cannot meet again. A *lendawe* was sung for Lina by an elderly Mamberamo woman who had cared for Dani in the Mamberamo region in 1977, teaching them how to process sago and make canoes, before journeying together to PNG. This *lendawe* retraces the mourner's relationship with Dani people through the activities that they undertook in certain places on their journey, and regrets that they will not retrace the journey home together:

> You arrived at our place
> starving, suffering
> we gave you food

showed you how to mattock sago to cook sago
to make a canoe
together we came to this place
O you have left us before we could return home
you have abandoned us in this foreign place which is not ours.

A year after Lina's death in September 2000, her friends (86 WPIA members) were repatriated to Wamena, leaving behind about 100 Dani at East Awin. Lina's friends might have assessed *merdeka* to be truly imminent, for Morning Star flags flew on almost every corner of Wamena town and outlying villages. At the time of their flight in 1977, raising the flag risked death by shooting, and enunciating the word 'Papua' was considered separatist. The appearance of reformation was to be short-lived though. On 6 October 2000, a military order was issued to lower Morning Star flags flying in the township of Wamena. Four were lowered and their flagpoles chopped down. At the fifth flag, soldiers were met with resistance and a physical clash and riot ensued. Soldiers killed independence supporters who killed migrants. Houses were incinerated, migrants fled for their lives, Dani were arbitrarily detained and subjected to torture, and a civilian curfew was imposed. For Lina's friends newly returned to Wamena after 23 years away, these events would have evoked the violence of 1977 from which they had initially fled as a terrifying allegory. The illusion of returning to a Dani homeland as it existed prior to aggressive military occupation in 1977 was shattered.

WPIA members had planned their repatriation to Irian Jaya during 1998–2000, a period promoted later as one of reformation or *reformasi* by the Wahid national government. To explain the intervening events that led to the riot, I have drawn extensively from Mote and Rutherford's meticulous chronology and analysis of events surrounding the Wamena incident.[8] The approach of President Wahid, and the previous President Habibie, was to promote dialogue with a West Papuan leadership through forums like the Team of One Hundred meeting, and the Second Papuan National Congress. Wahid's approach was also felt at the street level. He gave permission for the Morning Star flag to fly (albeit 30 centimetres below the Indonesian one), and he accepted the change of name from Irian Jaya to Papua. People raised the flag throughout the district of Jayawijaya, including Wamena. This district is a military operation zone, and hub of OPM activity, and its peoples have sustained the vast majority of human rights violations that have occurred in the province. An official tour to Wamena by Wahid's Deputy President Megawati Sukarnoputri in May 2000 was characterised by self-righteous and volatile crowds: 'at the airport … the vice president found herself facing a sea of Papuans waving the Morning Star flag, yelling at her to go home unless she had come to grant them independence.'[9]

Sukarnoputri and other members of an anti-Wahid coalition joined forces against Wahid, and forced him to act against West Papuan separatism. Additional Indonesian troops were sent to Irian Jaya, and the chief of police (reportedly at the demand of Sukarnoputri) ordered local police commanders across the province to remove all Morning Star flags. While the operation of the order was postponed at the request of the Papuan Presidium Council, in Wamena the authorities forcibly cut down and removed the Morning Star flag throughout the township and arrested and imprisoned 80 people. According to Mote and Rutherford, security forces fired shots over the crowd, and then fled into a migrant neighbourhood as a tactic to bring independence supporters face to face with migrants, thereby provoking a melee. The violence perpetrated against migrants was provoked in part by the violent treatment of independence supporters by the police immediately prior to the riot. Five days after the incident, Sukarnoputri's Security Minister Bambang Yudoyono (who won the Indonesian Presidency from Sukarnoputri in September 2004) set in train a process to develop a set of policies that would crush the independence movement. These included the banning of the Morning Star flag and an inquiry into the Papuan Presidium Council.

The melee aftermath resonates with the idea of sequences of actions that reverberate outward and upward through other 'cascades' of events.[10] The melee was invigorated by a collective history of Dani suffering in the Baliem. It caused local issues involving Dani people and police in Jayapura to be energised, imploding into various forms of violence.[11] These include the attack on a police post resulting in the death of two policemen and a security guard, a raid on several Dani student hostels and housing settlements resulting in the death of four Dani in police custody, the shooting to death of 10 people during a flag-raising ceremony in Jayapura and the flight of some 460, mainly Dani, asylum seekers into PNG.[12]

Following the flight of asylum seekers, PNG closed its border with Indonesia and increased patrols.[13] PNG Prime Minister Mekere Morauta reiterated his government's support of Indonesian sovereignty over Irian Jaya, and added that PNG would accept refugees from Irian Jaya only if the UN requested it to do so.[14] In the PNG press, the same arguments about border-crossers and political refugees were reiterated, and in the Cabinet, ministers resisted attempts to recognise the group as refugees and questioned how many OPM fighters lived among them.

The West Papuans camped initially at the Wutung border post, but were relocated to the previous site of the Blackwater refugee settlement near Vanimo by the Sandaun provincial government after protests by Wutung villagers. UNHCR did not consider them to have a prima facie claim to refugee status and encouraged the PNG government to determine their status individually.[15] The

PNG government granted them temporary protection on a humanitarian basis.[16] Later, in consultation with UNHCR, the government conducted refugee status determinations. It was reported that UNHCR recommended approximately 75 per cent be accorded refugee status.[17] The PNG Department of Foreign Affairs subsequently reassessed the claims, and granted refugee status to only 6 out of the 96 families. Initially the government sought the return of the 90 families to Indonesia on a voluntary basis, but later permitted them to remain indefinitely in the transmitter camp at Vanimo.

In March 2004, the 'Vanimo group' was recognised by the PNG government as refugees, and plans were made to relocate them to East Awin. Like those refugees at Vanimo in 1987, the group raised their voice in protest at relocation to East Awin. Letters were published on the internet news site 'The diary of online Papuan mouthpiece'. Invoking East Awin as a dystopic place, one writer wrote that the group: 'do not want to move, as they know already that Kiunga [i.e., East Awin] is the hell for them. Whoever sent there have never come back alive.' The site was an 'open prison for anyone from this Papua Soil.'[18] Under 15A of the Migration Act, the refugee group was required to relocate to East Awin where they could apply for permissive residency after six months of residence. The relocation exercise was held up by negotiations with Awin landholders and by the Vanimo group themselves who resisted relocation. Reflecting their security concerns as a minority, the landholders agreed to the resettlement of the Vanimo group after negotiating a law and order deal with the government: deployment of two policemen and one patrol officer at East Awin.[19] There had been no police presence at East Awin since the December incident in 1998.

On 1 October 2004, the Vanimo group comprising 360 people was airlifted to Kiunga by officials of the PNG government and UNHCR. The Vanimo group's Filadelfia Church was burned during the operation. Fearing the fate of their church, the refugee congregation had previously surrendered custody of it into the hands of the Catholic Bishop of Vanimo in a public ceremony. A UNHCR official advised PNG government officials that the church be respected as the custody of the Vanimo Diocese, and that the houses in the refugee settlement be dismantled rather than incinerated. Government officials reported that after the houses had been bulldozed, neighbouring villagers had burned the dismantled houses and airborne ash had ignited the thatched roof of the Filadelphia Church. Doubtless, other fallout would result when this news circulated among the Vanimo group and the wider refugee population at East Awin. The PNG government's refusal to recognise the Vanimo group as refugees until four years after their arrival is similar to the government's refusal to recognise West Papuans as refugees during the period 1984–87, and the burning of the Filadelphia Church in suspicious circumstances despite the public transfer of its custody to the

Vanimo Diocese is similar to the earlier burning of the Immanuel Church at Vanimo in 1989.

The arrival at East Awin of the Vanimo group may have served to confirm the perception that the state of *merdeka* is the only state that will guarantee freedom in the event of return. It is feasible that refugees at East Awin will retell the instance of Dani repatriation in allegorical terms, that is, the present is interpreted in terms of the lessons learned from similar events that have occurred in the past.[20] The repatriation carries the same lessons as 1977: highland peoples' resistance to the Indonesian state will be met by punitive retaliation and increased militarisation of the Baliem Valley. The entry of 360 new refugees, just two months after the exit of 630 others, underlines the volatility of the political situation in the Indonesian Province of Papua. Against a backdrop of refugee exit and refugee entry, repatriation might come to be seen by refugees as a circular experience.

Prospective repatriates may have been deterred by first-hand news of the treatment of West Papuans circulated by the arrivals from Vanimo in 2004.[21] Continued political repression in the Indonesian province of Papua vivifies a West Papuan collective 'memory of suffering' or *memoria passionis* in the present. To return to the province into this milieu of fear that is constantly reproduced[22] is to dispense with the object of exile: to live outside a state of terror, and for some, to struggle for the elimination of terror in a state of *merdeka*. With *merdeka* no longer perceived to be imminent, repatriation is out of the question—but return is not. Projecting in terms of the cosmology of refugee subjects, I would propose that over time permissive residency itself may come to be experienced as a sort of 'godsend'. By offering mobility to West Papuan refugees, everyday connections to the homeland can be sustained from a viable and safe place across the border in PNG.

ENDNOTES

[1] Keagop, 'Upaya terakhir kembali ke tanah air', *Jubi* 11, 1319 September 2000, pp. 3–4.

[2] Keagop, 'Suara pengungsi, suara kegelisahan', *Jubi* 11, 1319 September 2000, pp. 5–6.

[3] Chris Duncan, 'From development to empowerment: changing Indonesian government policies towards peripheral minorities', unpublished manuscript, n. d.

[4] R. A. Tucker, *From Jerusalem to Irian Jaya: a biographical history of Christian missions*, Academic Books, Michigan, 1983.

[5] B. Giay and J. A. Godschalk, 'Cargoism in Irian Jaya today', *Oceania*, 63, 1993, pp. 330–44.

[6] Kirsch, 'Changing views'.

[7] Giay, *Menuju Papua Baru,* pp. 9–10.

[8] Mote and Rutherford, pp. 121–3.

[9] Mote and Rutherford, p. 122.

[10] Appadurai, p. 151.

[11] Appadurai, p. 164.

[12] Jayapura Secretariat for Justice and Peace, 'Peristiwa Tragedi Kemanusiaan Wamena 6 Oktober 2000, Sebelum dan Sesudahnya, Januari 2001', <http://www.hampapua.org/skp/skp06/var-02i.pdf>

[13] US Committee for Refugees, 'Papua New Guinea: World Refugee Survey 2001 Country Report', <http://www.refugees.org/world/countryrpt/easia_pacific/2001/papua_new_guinea.htm>

[14] US Committee for Refugees, 'Papua New Guinea: World Refugee Survey 2003 Country Report'.

[15] US Committee for Refugees, 'Papua New Guinea: World Refugee Survey 2001 Country Report'.

[16] US Committee for Refugees, 'Papua New Guinea: World Refugee Survey 2001 Country Report'.

[17] International Commission of Jurists and The Refugee Council of Australia, paragraphs 310, 311, 319, 320.

[18] WP News, 'West Papuan refugees asking the Vanuatu Prime Minister to remove them to Vanuatu', 24 September 2004, *West Papua News dot com*, <http://www.westpapuanews.com/articles/publish/article_1281.shtml>

[19] Johann Siffointe, UNHCR Liaison Office Port Moresby, pers. comm., November 2004.

[20] Malkki, p. 106.

[21] Treatment of West Papuans since 2001 is elaborated in reports published by the Memoria Passionis series of the Catholic Diocese of Jayapura's Office of Justice and Peace <http://www.hampapua.org/skp/>

[22] Michael Taussig, *Shamanism, colonialism and the wild man: a study in terror and healing*, University of Chicago Press, Chicago, 1987.

Coda

Forty-three West Papuans arrive in Australia by outrigger canoe, 2006

Seven years after completing fieldwork at East Awin, the arrival of 43 West Papuans by outrigger canoe accorded a certain currency to that fieldwork. The event of the arrival and the subsequent processing of asylum claims and issuing of temporary visas focused intense media and public attention on foreign policy relations between Australia and Indonesia.

This book offers another 'frame' through which to view the 2006 outrigger landing, for West Papuans have crossed boundaries to seek asylum since 1962, usually eastward into PNG and occasionally southward to Australia. This coda does not set out to provide new material, but draws on the published work of other historians of West Papuan displacement, namely, Stuart Kirsch, Richard Chauvel, Klaus Neumann and David Palmer.[1]

There are many more internally displaced Papuans than there are Papuans who have crossed international boundaries to seek asylum. An estimated 20,000 Papuans have been internally displaced during the period 2001–06, and much of this displacement has occurred in the Central Highlands region. The 2001 Law on Special Autonomy for Papua created new administrative units that required additional military and police commands. Classified as a 'military operations area', the Indonesian Province of Papua hosts Indonesian security forces including army troops, police units and mobile paramilitary police. 'Sweeping' operations including checkpoints, roadblocks and raids have been conducted by Indonesian security forces to expose OPM members and supporters. Such operations have been documented by researchers in the following places: Wasior (2001), Kiyawage area (2003), Tolikara regency (January–March 2005), and Puncak Jaya (2004; August–October 2005; December 2006).

Demographic change resulting in segmentation and stratification of the population causes street-level tensions between indigenous Papuans and migrants. More than 500,000 spontaneous migrants have migrated to the Province of Papua, and continue to arrive.[2] (This figure does not include the estimated 220,000 transmigrants who arrived until the late 1990s.) While Indonesian migrant-dominated urban areas in Papua have become integrated into the modern economy of Indonesia, the interior, particularly the highlands where the majority of indigenous Papuans live, remains an isolated subsistence economy. Chauvel's analysis is insightful.[3] He describes the spatial separation of the Indonesian settler and Papuan economies, and the meeting of these economies in the marketplace, which has become segmented, stratified and volatile. Violent clashes have been documented in markets in Hamadi (1984), Entrop (2000) and Abepura (2000). This book has documented the way that macro-level violence can cause repercussions that spread and become folded into local politics.[4]

Political conflict in Papua leading to internal and international displacement has been elaborated by the historians mentioned above. The UNHCR also articulates this relation in explicit terms, its 2006 Country Operations Plan advising: 'Its [PNG's] proximity and cultural ties to the Indonesian province of Papua means there is potential for a mass influx of West Papuan refugees. Given the continuing political instability and the security situation in Papua, regular revision of PNG's contingency plans and training of PNG officials is considered important.'[5]

It has been easterly movement across the border into PNG rather than southward movement to Australia that has characterised the pattern of movement for West Papuans seeking asylum. The movement of West Papuans out of the former UNHCR settlement at East Awin in Western Province, Papua New Guinea, has not been southward either. Rather, West Papuans have tended to relocate to the nearest mining town in Western Province, or to the border town of Vanimo in Sandaun Province. A few families have made secondary movement from Vanimo westward to the capital Jayapura.

Any further southward movement to Australia by West Papuans would occur in spite of intense sea-patrolling activity and punitive legislation discriminating against boat arrivals seeking asylum.

One of the curious effects of the issue of temporary protection visas to the outrigger canoe arrivals by the Howard Government, was that at the time of the expiry of the visas in around 2009, the Department of Immigration would have been required to determine whether the Indonesian Province of Papua was a durably safe place to which the West Papuans might, or might not be returned. It is unlikely that either assessment would have surprised West Papuans living in PNG. If it was determined that Papua was a durably safe place to which West Papuan asylum seekers might be repatriated, then it would be understood that Indonesia–Australian foreign policy relations had been privileged, and if it had been determined that Papua was not a durably safe place then this assessment would validate West Papuans' rationale for remaining in PNG.

In May 2008, the Rudd Government abolished the temporary protection visa regime for asylum seekers. This meant that, along with some 1000 other refugees on temporary visas who met ´security and character requirements´, the 43 West Papuans would be entitled to permanent protection visas allowing for permanent residency in Australia.[6]

ENDNOTES

[1] Richard Chauvel, 'Refuge, displacement and dispossession: responses to Indonesian rule and conflict in Papua', in E. E. Hedman (ed.) *Dynamics of conflict and displacement in Papua, Indonesia*, Refugee Studies Centre Working Paper No. 42, 2007, pp.32–51; Stuart Kirsch, 'Representations of violence, conflict, and displacement in West Papua', in E. E. Hedman (ed.), pp. 52–68; Klaus Neumann, *Refuge Australia: Australia's humanitarian record*, UNSW Press, Sydney, 2004; David Palmer, 'Between a rock and a hard place: the case of Papuan asylum-seekers', *Australian Journal of Politics and History*, 52, 4, 2006, pp. 576–603.

[2] McGibbon 2004, p. 23, in Chauvel p. 34.

[3] Chauvel, pp. 35–6.

[4] Rosenau in Appadurai, pp. 152–3.

[5] Chauvel, pp. 41–2.

[6] http://www.minister.immi.gov.au/media/media-releases/2008/ce05-buget-08.htm (15 June 2008).

www.ingramcontent.com/pod-product-compliance
Lightning Source LLC
Chambersburg PA
CBHW061222270326
41927CB00022B/3458